Animated Stills

Poetic Pareidolia

Inspiration of Life from Photographs

Thomas G Reischel

Word Art Publishing
9350 Wilshire Blvd
Suite 203, Beverly Hills, CA 90212
www.wordartpublishing.com
Phone: 1 (888) 614 - 1370

Published by Word Art Publishing

ISBN: 978-1-955070-73-7 (Hardcover)
ISBN: 978-1-955070-64-5 (Paperback)
ISBN: 978-1-955070-65-2 (eBook)

Dedication

I dedicate this book to my brother Richard, who enjoyed my poetry, but died too young in July of 2018. Like the Phoenix, may his spirit soar now in the heights.

Acknowledgements

I'd like to thank my wife, Karen Lynne (Sweetnam) Reischel, for her patience and acceptance of my time spent working on this book. Thanks to all the support staff at the Publisher, for making the process simple and easy. This book would not have been possible if it were not for the site where I post all my poems, FanStory, and where each poem gets reviewed by my peer poets. Many thanks to Wikipedia as a profound source of knowledge. Plus all my other fans, family and friends. I fully appreciate your time and support.

Introduction

Animated Stills: Poetic Pareidolia

This book is an Inspiration of Life from photographs.

As a photographer, I roam around and take pictures of many things. Some of those pictures contain images where I see something in them. As a Poet, this sparks my imagination, my Muse, to poetically interpret that "something" into action. So a poem is born. I write about it, and ask the readers if they see it too. I think that it's fun. We are exercising Pareidolia.

Pareidolia (par-i-DOH-lee-a) is the tendency to interpret a vague stimulus as something known to the observer, such as seeing shapes in clouds, seeing faces in inanimate objects or abstract patterns, or hearing hidden messages in music.

Common examples are perceived images of animals, faces, or objects in cloud formations, the Man in the Moon, the Rorschach Ink Blot tests, hidden messages in recorded music when played in reverse, and hearing indistinct voices in random noise such as that produced by air conditioners or fans.

That is the basis of this book of Animated Stills. The "stills" part comes from the photograph. The "animated" portion is where poet brings the perceived image to life for the reader. Animated stills are poems where inanimate objects take on human, animal, or spirit forms, traits, or articles. They are derived from Photographs I have taken, that have moved me to write a poem associated with it.

I believe that photography and poetry go together well. One form paints a visual picture while the other creates a poetic image. Together, the synergy becomes very powerful. At least, that is what I hope I have achieved here. This book contains both, with a twist – a hidden reveal. All the photographs contained in this book were taken by the author and the poetry was also written by him. The photos were all taken within the state. So, besides the esthetic journey, I hope the book also provides the reader a bit of information about the place that is my home.

So, this book is very much a picture book. As a photographer, I present the image to you. Without the image, the poem would not exist. It becomes a flight of imagination expressed in poetry. In that sense, it is meant to be a fun fantasy of shared experience. We connect. Then, from that static still-life comes a story brought to life. The inanimate becomes animated. This book contains 75 original photographs taken by the author himself. Some pictures have such an impact on me, that I used it more than once.

As an author, my job is to point out the perception some way. To bring you into my imagination, where we journey together. In the end, the reader says, "Yes, I see it too!" We share a smile. This author resides in St. Paul, Minnesota, USA. The reader can be anywhere in the world. Yet we touched each other somehow.

As a Poet, I use every technique I can to express the thought captured in that image, and bring about the concept that the picture inspired. It may just reveal the hidden mystery, point out a surprising fact, recall something from history, generate some humor, or even launch into a story. I use different formats to create these poems. This book contains 75 poems written in 52 different formats. Each poem identifies its format right below the title. See the Descriptions of Poetic Formats and Glossary of Poetry Types at the back of the book for further details.

Many people have read books of poetry, and either like it or not, based on how they felt after the read. But few have known what really hides behind the words on the page. And that's a shame, because part of what creates the ultimate feeling the reader gets is due to a number of poetic techniques the poet used. Unless they are shown those, it really goes unperceived. I try to remedy that here in this book too.

Besides the poem itself, the author will typically add author's notes. These notes generally try to provide three bits of information. First will be a comment about the poem itself. Second, a description of the poetic format is provided. Finally, the author may comment about the photograph. All this is provided to be informational. It may be redundant or unnecessary for some. Those individuals can skip over what they want, part or even all of the notes. They are there for those who appreciate them, and want to go further into what is behind just the words.

To understand this book better, a number of technical items must be addressed. If you already know these things, just skip this area.

Let's start with a discussion of rhyme. Poems may or may not have rhyme. Although, most Sonnets do rhyme. The rhyme is usually at the end of each line and is known as "End-rhyme". If not at the end, it is known as "In-line rhyme". As you read my poetic descriptions, I may refer to the End-rhymes in an alphanumeric code. For example, the first rhyming word in a poem is referred to as the "a" rhyme, and every line in the poem that rhymes with it is designated the letter "a". The second rhyme to occur would be identified as "b", the third as "c", and so on. The most common poem has 4 lines (a Quatrain). The most typical End-rhyme schemes for a Quatrain are:

> aabb (Coupled Rhyme)
> abab (Alternating Rhyme)
> abba (Enveloping Rhyme)
> abcb (Skipping Rhyme)

Beyond End-line and In-line Rhyme are other nuances. For example, there may be no End-line Rhymes, but lines rhyme within the middle of each line. This is known as Hidden Rhyme. A very Welsh adaptation is known as Cross Rhyme, where the End-line Rhyme matches to an In-line word on the following line. Rhymes can also be identified as perfect, near, or slant.

> Perfect Rhyme is where the stressed vowel sound between two words are identical, plus any subsequent sounds.

Near Rhyme is a rhyme between a stressed and an unstressed syllable – wing/caring.

Slant Rhyme is rhyme matching assonance (vowels) or consonance –shake/hate or rabies/robbers.

Oblique Rhyme is rhyme where the sounds are similar, but don't really match – one/thumb, or green/fiend.

Syllabic Rhyme is rhyme in which the last syllable sound the same, but are not the stressed syllable – pitter/patter.

Mono-rhyme is where all the End-line rhymes in a stanza, (or even the entire multi-stanza poem) are the same.

No Rhyme is known as Free Verse or Blank Verse, although Free Verse with some rhyme is known as Free Style.

Now, let's turn from rhymes to line structure. There are many other line structures in poetry besides the Quatrain, based on the number of lines. Simply speaking, the most common are:

Two lines – a Couplet
Three lines – a Tercet
Four lines – a Quatrain
Five lines – a Quintain, or a Quintet, or Cinquain
Six lines – a Sestet, or Sexain, or Sextet
Seven lines – a Septet, or Septain
Eight lines – an Octave, or Octet
Nine Lines – a Nanotet, or Nonet, or a Spenserian Stanza
Ten lines – a Decatain, or Decatet, or Decastitch
Twelve lines – Duodecatain
Fouteeen lines – typically, a Sonnet

Poems may contain a paragraph. These are known as Stanzas. These Stanzas may contain the same rhyme or may vary. In order to distinguish the Rhyme Scheme, an alphanumeric code is typically employed. Here are examples of the Rhyme Scheme of a poem with two Stanzas.

aabb baba (Here the rhyme was the same in both, but one was coupled while the other was alternating).

aabb ccdd (Here each stanza has two different coupled rhymes)

Poems may also contain one or more repeating rhyme. That means it has the same identical rhyme word. This is usually identified using a capital letter, like so:

Abab Abab (Here I'm referring to the first rhyme of each stanza being repeated)

It could also mean a complete repeating of an entire line or Refrain. That would be identified in the author's notes. Sometimes the Refrain is referred to with the letter "R." In either case the Rhyme or Refrain may be interlocking. Below are two examples of interlocking Tercets. The first interlocks the rhyme or refrain of the first line of each stanza, while in the second, the middle letter creates the rhyme for the next stanza.

Abc **A**de **A**fg
a**B**a b**C**b c**D**c ded

A similar treatment can be achieved by interlocking Quatrains with a Couplet, as follows:

aa**B**a bb**C**b cc**D**c dd

Speaking of repeated Refrains,(which can be a word, an entire line, or part of a line), different treatments can create different effects. Here are as examples of some Refrain effects you will see here in the Sonnets.

Waterfall – **A**bab c**A**ca ad**A**d a**A** (the A ripples through moving one position in each stanza)
Sustained – **A**bab **A**cac **A**dad **A**a (the A remains in the same first line of each stanza)
Echo – aba**B** cdc**B** ded**B** b**B** (the B remains the last line of each stanza)
Double Envelope – **AB**ab cdcd efef **AB** (first two lines become last two)
Reverse Double Envelop – **AB**ab cdcd efef **BA** (same, but Couplet reversed)
Double Summary – **A**ba**B** cdcd efef **AB** (first and last lime of stanza become last lines of poem)
Reverse Double Summary- **A**ba**B** cdcd efef **BA** (same as other, but Couplet reversed)
Stanzaic – **A**bab **C**dcd efef **AC** First line of first two stanzas become closing Couplet
Reverse Stanzaic –**A**bab **C**dcd efef **CA** (same, but Couplet reversed)
Rolling – **ABCD A**bab **B**cbc **C**dcd **D**ede (All first stanza lines create subsequent sequential firsts)

Poems can mix Stanza styles. For example, an English Sonnet often contains 3 Quatrains and a Couplet (14 total lines), while an Italian Sonnet contains an Octave and a Sestet (also 14 lines).

Furthermore, poems also may contain a structured syllable count. This establishes the rhythm at which the poem is read, which is known as Meter. Typically these are paired in sets of two, known as a foot. There is a name for each type of Meter, as follows.
Two syllables - Monometer (one foot)
Four syllables - Dimeter (two Feet)
Six syllables - Trimeter (three feet)
Eight syllables - Tetrameter (four feet)
Ten syllables - Pentameter (five feet)
Twelve syllables – Hexameter or Alexandrian (six feet)
Fourteen syllables - Heptameter (seven feet)
Sixteen Syllables - Octameter (eight feet)

The ones most common or frequently used are Tetrameter and Pentameter.

The most complex poetic concept focuses around syllable accents, whether they are hard or soft, and how they are linked together. The most common of these are iambic and the trochaic (trochee) Meters. As you speak a word, there is an accent on each syllable that results in either a soft or a hard sound. For example the word cowboy puts the hard accent on the first syllable – **COW**boy. The word police, puts the hard accent on the second syllable – po**LICE**. How you string words together determines the type of Meter. Iambic Meter alternates soft -hard, soft- hard. For example, Shakespeare's famous words –"To be or not to be" is iambic: to **BE** or **NOT** to **BE**. But the second half is not iambic – **THAT** is the **QUES**tion. Iambic is frequently defined as da-Dum, da-DUM type Meter, where each da-Dum is a poetic foot. Therefore, Iambic Pentameter would carry a Meter of: da-**DUM**, da-**DUM**, da-**DUM**, da-**DUM**, da-**DUM**.

I should mention something here about Feminine Iambic Meter. Most Iambic Meters contain an even number of syllable counts (2,4,6,8,10,12,14), with the hard accent on the second, or last, syllable. But, a feminine line adds an extra syllable that ends on a soft accent (for example, a one word line – eMOtion – is an example of Feminine Iambic Monometer). As a rule, when there is one line of Feminine Iambic Meter, there should be a matching second line paired with it in some manner.
Trochee is exactly the opposite of iambic, where each line starts with a hard syllable accent and ends with a soft.
 TWINkle **TWIN**kle **LIT**tle **STAR**,
 HOW I **WON**der **WHAT** you **ARE**.

An item unique to a Sonnet, Senryu, or Haiku, is a Volta, or turn. That occurs where the poem is leading you in one direction, then suddenly surprises you with a change. In Sonnets, the usual place for a Volta is at the 9th line. Often, it is strongly demarked with words like: but, still, yet, oh, and alas. Sometimes it is more subtle. Recognizing the Volta can become an added joy in reading a poem.

I hope readers will appreciate my pointing these things out as it is not my intention to bore them, but rather I hope it may bring additional depth of appreciation to the poetry. If not, feel free to skip over that part.

Well, that's about as deep as I want to get about poetry techniques.

So, this book is really meant for several types of readers. There will be those who merely want to see the photographs. I think that is wonderful, and hope that my photography is sufficiently good enough to satisfy their craving. Others will just like the poetry. Again, although I don't purport to be an expert, I hope that I have at least accomplished some success and have whetted their appetite for more. Some may want to focus on style and format, and I believe this book should appeal to them as well.

The unique interplay of the Pareidolia aspects of this book is meant to add a further dimension that is both playful, and revealing. My hope is that it brings joy, astonishment, and imagination to the reader.

In addition, I hope this book becomes a learning tool for some. I believe that it might appeal to both poetry teachers, as well as poetry students. To that end, I have added a lot of information about poetic techniques. This book contains examples of different types, or formats, if you will. I have included a Glossary of Poetry Types that I used at the back of this book.

There are 13 Chapters. The chapters have been organized by the category, then in alphabetical order of the poem's title. There are chapters about the environment, evil, historical artifacts, humor, intriguing observations, myths, religion, revealed mysteries, season, shocking discoveries, and surprising sights.

I think you'll find that these pages have some amazing photographs.

I hope you enjoy the poetry that my imagination pulled from those images.

Maybe you will learn some things about poetry that you didn't appreciate before. The author doesn't claim to be an authority in these areas, so please allow him a bit of poetic license.

Finally, I would be delighted if you enjoyed the fun of finding those "faces in the clouds."

Table of Contents

Chapter 1 – Comedy

This chapter shows the humor that can even be found in nature. These inanimate objects can truly be funny. Hopefully, you might smile, or even get a laugh. What better way to start a book, than that? To explore the comedy in the surroundings. We can laugh together. For laughter is a universal language. There are thousands of languages and even more dialects, but everyone speaks laughter, and when you're smiling "the whole world smiles with you."

In this chapter, the personalities of trees and rocks capture the spotlight. There's a tree with a foot, trees with odd bends, one that hides a shy bird, one that scares away armed men, one with a most unusual trunk, and one very sassy tease. There is also a rock exercising.

So see for yourself. Read, look, and see if you too can say, "Yes, I see it!" Then let's smile together.

Poem 1: Best Foot
(AABB Quatrains)

Even if you're wrinkled with age,

And your Life has reached the Ancient Age,

And you have a tangled Root

Put forward your Best Foot

Author Notes:

I couldn't resist this obvious subject taken from a root found along the Mississippi River bank near Harriet Island. Doesn't it really look like a tree with a foot? I just had to pen this verse. Hope you like it.

This poem is AABB Quatrains
These are poems written in a standard 4 line stanza (Quatrain) with a rhyme scheme of aabb (coupled).

Poem 2: Crooked Trees
(A Limerick Sonnet)

The trees on our block have grown crooked.
Their chance to be stately don't look it.
But is it way too late
to make them grow straight?
To test each, we went up and shook it.

Each tree trunk was as solid as steel.
Their profile is something quite unreal.
But taking them out
ain't what I'm about.
I hope to restore their appeal.

Oh wait! I just read in a book,
that's how Japanese make them look.

Well, what do you know?
They don't have to go!

Author Notes:

You Know, those are Japanese Bonsai Trees. I found these along a boulevard at Lake Nokomis I Minneapolis, Mn.

This poem is a Limerick Sonnet.
According to the dictionary, a Limerick Form consists of 5 Lines (two long, followed by two short, and closed by 1 long). The first, second and fifth Lines must have matching lengths of seven to ten Syllables (8 or 9 is most typical). The third and fourth Lines only
have between five and seven Matching Syllables. So there is a bit of flexibility.

The long Cadence is either: da DUM da da DUM da da DuM da; or, da DUM da da DUM da da DUM.
The short cadence is either: da DUM da da DUM; or, da DUM da da DUM da.

The Limerick Sonnet uses a Quintet (5 line) structure with two Closing Couplets rather than one, in order to achieve the classic 14 lines. The Volta comes at the first Couplet
(lines 11 and 12).
The Rhyme Scheme is:
 aabba ccddc ee ff.
The syllable count is:
9,9,5,5,9 – 8,8,5,5,8- 9,9 – 5,5.

19

Poem 3: Shy Sheldon the Shoo Shoo Bird

(A Nonsense Poem)

There was a shy bird who said "Shoo,"
it wasn't a "Hoo", but a "Shoo."
Because he was shy,
and couldn't quite fly,
he would hide in the woods that he knew,
behind rocks and some trees,
one or two.

He was scared of the shadow he threw.
Which was when that his feathers turned blue.
And you knew, he would wish us adieu.
If you spot him, you'll hear "Shoo Shoo Shoo"
Shoo Shoo Shoo
Shoo Shoo Shoooo

You may never, have ever, have heard
of this timid and sneaky old bird
He is so very shy
I don't even know why
it really is simply absurd
He won't speak, if you please
Not a word

He is Sheldon the shy Shoo Shoo Bird
Not a peep, or a chirp, will be heard,
Not a cackle, or tweet, or a hoo.
Our Sheldon will only say "Shoo,"
Shoo Shoo Shoo
Shoo Shoo Shoo
Shoo Shoo Shoooo

Author's Notes:

Don't worry! If you never heard of a Shoo Shoo Bird, it's because I just made it up for this poem. I created this poem from the picture. I hope you see, like I do, the image of a bird in that stump on the left of the tree trunk. It looked to me like it was peeking shyly around the trunk, as if it was trying to hide, or at least blend in

The poem is just a Nonsense Poem for children. I tried to give a Dr, Seuss feel to it. A Nonsense Poem is a long established tradition in creative writing and is still popular with readers of English language poems. Poetry that has no real meaning and often makes us laugh and think weird things has a unique appeal. A form of nonsense literature usually employing strong prosodic elements like rhythm and rhyme. It is whimsical and humorous in tone and employs some of the techniques of nonsense literature. Limericks are probably the best known form of nonsense verse, although they tend nowadays to be used for bawdy or straightforwardly humorous, rather than nonsensical, effect. Some poems use made up words to describe things, or just to make a nice sound. Lewis Carroll, Edward Lear and Spike Milligan are good authors to read if you like nonsense poetry.

Poem 4: Stumped
(Sonnet, English)

Within dark Forest deep, they blithely walked
Surrounded by beauty most fine. Devine!
Two Troubadours ambled along and talked
With mellow cheer, time passed, imbibing wine.

When suddenly silhouettes clearly became
A sight that was lurking nearby the path.
The open maw and stance shows it's untame.
Would teeth unleash and rend with fearsome wrath?

They stopped! They Looked! Uncertain of their plan.
Do alligators live in yonder park?
Brave fellows that they were, well-armed - they Ran!
Such terrors seem much worse there in the Dark.

Two Troubadours turned into craven chumps!
Terrorized! Quaking! Frightened by some stumps!

Author Notes:

Brave men indeed. This is another poem that requires the image of a tree stump. When I came across this stump, it gave me pause too, and inspired this poem. A simple story of some drunken troubadours traveling in the forest told as in sonnet format.

This poem is an English Sonnet.
A traditional English Sonnet is a poem of 14 lines. It follows a strict Rhyme Scheme. It is often about love. It consists of 14 lines, each line containing ten Syllables and is written in iambic Pentameter, in which a pattern of an Unstressed Syllable followed by a Stressed Syllable is repeated five times. The rhyme scheme in a English Sonnet is:
a-b-a-b, c-d-c-d, e-f-e-f, g-g.
The last two lines are a Rhyming Couplet.

Poem 5: Take a Bough
(1-9-1 Poem)

Tree
A Shady Oak with Junk in the Trunk
Mooned

Author Notes:

I just couldn't resist this one.
My photograph. Taken September 2012 at Big Bog State Park, Red Lake, Minnesota.
Mooned - American slang for dropping the trousers and flashing the buttocks, usually at a crowd. When both cheeks are large and fully exposed, it's called a full moon. Blushing allowed.

Junk in the Trunk - Black American slang for having a large posterior.

I guess the Bog wasn't the only thing that was big!

This poem is a 1-9-1 Poem
A 1-9-1 Poem is a three line poem that is syllabic. The first line has a word with only 1 syllable. The second line carries a phrase of nine syllables. The last and final line is back to 1 syllable. No meter. Rhyming is optional. Although short. This format can be quite expressive, especially when joined to a picture.

25

Poem 6: Turtle Doing Situps
(Quatrains, Mixed)

Stuck on ONE
Here's how it's begun.

The crow cried "Slow! Slow! Slow!"
"I can see how slow you go."
The turtle said, "What do you know?"
"It's the creator made me so!"

The crow cried, "No! No! No!"
"You have let your body fat grow!"
"That's what makes you go so slow!"
The turtle said, "Oh, I don't know!"

So the turtle went home and checked his weight.
It wasn't far. There isn't a gate.
He got on the scale, to his amazement found
That in the last week, he'd gained over a pound

That crow was right! There's something to it!
There's nothing to say but "Just get out and do it!"
"I'll have to do some heavy exercise
To keep myself healthy, wealthy, and wise"

So he put on his gym clothes and striped socks,
An he slowly climbed up on a pile of rocks,
He said, "A few sit-ups I think I'll try."
He rolled over on his heavy shell with a sigh.

And did what no other turtle had done

ONE

Author notes:

Whether Shell or Rock, It's Hard
This is just a silly Children's Poem
inspired by this picture of a rock. To me, it
looks like a Turtle doing a sit up. This
rock was just alongside a road near my
house in the landscape of a townhouse
complex. It just tickled my funny bone so I
had to create a story about this turtle that
will never get to two. I hope you see it.
Look for the head on the upper right side.

This poem is Mixed Quatrains with some
other additions as well.
Mixed, or Combination Format poems are
those that contain two or more poetic
formats.

Poem 7: Wicked Willow
(Tercets)

Hey baby! Look at me!
Aren't I a lovely willow tree!
I think I'm pretty sexy!

How many trees can lay like this?
Come on over! Give me a kiss!
I'll treat you to some woody bliss!

I'm out here on this beach,
So my bark can bray a sultry speech,
To bring you within my reach.

Here I am, right by the sand!
Green pom-pom in my pretty hand!
I think I look so very grand!

Don't you just love my shaggy top!
You think I'm easy? OH Stop!!
Before I call a cop!

Author Notes:

A poetic treatise on a real tree
tease! Just a little nonsense. Doesn't this
look just like a sassy pom-pom girl of a
tree?

I took this picture of a willow tree at Lake
Phalen in St. Paul, Minnesota in August
of 2012. Such an unusual tree. It
reminded me of a model posing. It even
has a belly button. So, this poem was
always waiting to come out. It finally did
as I was going through my photographs.

Chapter 2: Environmental

Here we have a set of poems that have an environmental aspect to aspect to them. The key thought throughout is that mankind has not been too kind to the earth, and that nature may someday have a reckoning. We note that the trees we cut are living things. Men go out to nature and disturb it, often leaving their trash as well. We hunt animals to extinction. Someone or something may be watching and waiting. So let's be good stewards of the environment.

Poem 8: Alien Attack Within
(Sestets)

When you come upon a tree,
There's more to it than you can see.
Its crown is high,
Its roots are deep,
Its leaves all flutter in the sky,
And secrets it will keep.

For it was planted long ago.
It's grown through heat and heavy snow.
It's observed for many years,
The good, the bad, the tears,
The rapid pace
Of the Human Race

The trees stood in silent horror,
Where for ages they had stood
As the earliest explorer,
Chopped down the virgin wood.
Now kindling for fires,
Lumber for lofty towers.

These ancient living souls
Were milled into single poles,
Some ground into paper books,
Cut at Christmas for their looks.
Blithely destroying living things
For the glory of their Kings

These ancient life-breathing forms
Will weather these human storms.
Finally upset by Human greed,
And disregard for Earth's great need,
They could gather to take the world back.
They could make an alien attack

To Maintain atmospheric clean air,
Oblivious Mankind beware!

Author Notes:

Mankind is continuing to blindly use up the earth's resources with disregard for the livings things they share this planet with. Nature has the power, and already has used it, to destroy civilizations. They disappear. Could this be another scenario? Maybe.

This photograph was taken along the shore of the Mississippi River, across from the city of St. Paul, Minnesota. This driftwood looked to my imagination like an alien insect scouting for an invasion army. Of course it just a tree, but they are living things that we abuse

This poem is a set of Sestets.
A Sestet is simply a poem with stanzas that have six lines.

The uneven flow is intentional

Poem 9: Angry Ancient Oaks
(A Sonnet, English)

The ancient oaks that guard this glen
Are jealous of the folks who come.
They're suspicious of where and when,
The stranger's past they're coming from.

'Fore they've been fooled by cheats before,
Of forest treasures come to steal,
To strip the wood and leave the floor
So barren, it took years to heal.

So, let them know that you're a friend.
Despoil not any sacred ground!
Leave only footprints in the end.
All else, leave as it was first found.

Then angry looks will turn to smiles,
And nature will rejoice for miles.

Author Notes

I was walking in the forest one morning at Lake Elmo Park Reserve in Minnesota, and came upon this glen of oak trees. They looked like they had angry faces and raised this poem out of me. Since the trees look alive to me,

This poem is an English Sonnet. A traditional English Sonnet is a poem of 14 lines. It follows a strict Rhyme Scheme. It is often about love. It consists of 14 lines, each line containing ten Syllables and is written in iambic Pentameter, in which a pattern of an Unstressed Syllable followed by a Stressed
Syllable is repeated five times. The rhyme scheme in a English Sonnet is:
a-b-a-b, c-d-c-d, e-f-e-f, g-g.
The last two lines are a Rhyming Couplet.

Poem 10: The Bruin Blend
(Hir a Thoddaid)

Once this land was the providence of bears.
Fierce and proud, they all wandered everywhere.
A fighting form, no other foe would dare
to take them on. In strength, none could compare.
For they could tear, and shred with mighty paws.
Their massive jaws and lethal claws impair.
But then a change came rolling in on wheels,
where unaware, the bear's fate now it seals,
as many men start hunting them for meals,
and for their coat. So warm and soft it feels,
it appeals to unbridled, endless lust.
And so bears must adjust to such ordeals.
Away from men, the bruins took to trees,
where they blend to the elements with ease.
The hunters look for them, but no one sees,
as bear coats blend, to the subtlest degrees,
with bark of trees. They hide among the roots,
whose attributes conceal them, where they've squeezed.

Author Notes:

Bears do blend in to their environment quite well, but this is actually just a tree root on Harriet Island by downtown St. Paul, Minnesota, that sure looks a lot like a bear, when viewed from the right angle. Providence - guided by nature, or God Subtlest is read as 3 syllables.

The format of this poem is a Hir a Thoddaid. A Hir a Thoddaid is a Welsh form of Awdl poetry. There are twelve Awdl forms. An Awdl is a Welsh ode. This form contains a ten syllable quatrain followed by a Thoddaid. A Hir is a set of four Isosyllabic (10 Syllables, no fixed meter) lines with the same mono-rhymed end line. A Thoddaid is the couplet with the cross rhyme aspect.
All lines of each stanza, except for the penultimate one, rhyme together in the conventional way. The penultimate line rhymes with them all in an unconventional way - an inline syllable. Furthermore, the word at the end of the penultimate line rhymes with a word somewhere in the middle of the last line. The Hir can have 6 lines, rather than the 4 used here, but all its lines must always mono-rhyme together. Frequently the stanzas are blended together without blank lines between, as I have chosen here, to give it a more Welsh feel.
the letters in parens show how the inline rhyme goes. Rhyme Scheme: aaaa(ab)(ba), where the letters in parens show how the inline rhyme goes.

Poem 11: The Watching Whistler
(Septets)

Along the River banks they lurk.
The Ancient ones of Earth
They whistle, watch and smirk
At all Humanity's civic work.
They often wonder at the worth
Of cutting all their fellow Trees
That once swayed here in the breeze.

Author Notes

Nature Confronts Civilization.
I *certainly* see a tree root casually watching and whistling. I wondered just what it was thinking. This Photograph was taken along the Mississippi River at Harriet Island. This is an undoctored image. The root actually looks like that. The City in the background is St. Paul which is directly across the river.

This poem is a Septet
A Septet is simply a poem with 7 lines of any style, format, or meter.

Chapter 3: Evil

If evil exists, and I'm sure it does, can it be seen around us? I'm sure it can

Here are some poems to prove it. There is one about a haunted forest. Another shows how Satan has a grip on the world. The demons may even have a portal into our world from the depths of hell.

As you observe what goes on in today's world, through news happening worldwide, one can't but conclude that evils have been unleashed in a massive way. Many feel we are in the end times as described in the bible. Others believe Global Warming will destroy us in the next 10 years. Then there is always contagions that are being unleashed. Maybe we will destroy ourselves in a nuclear conflagration. All aspects of Evil.

I certainly don't cover them all, but here are a few examples I encountered.

41

Poem 12: Beware the Trees

(A Tambour)]

A forest glade with trees and shade, and travel trampled path
may harbor hosts of ghouls and ghosts, or hidden psychopaths.
For danger lurks in old earthworks concealed within the grass.
One seldom sees but even trees are hostile to trespass.
It's understood that even wood can contain an evil strain
that holds a grudge when strangers trudge within their harsh domain.
Unbidden, unwanted, traveler's tales say they're haunted
where only the bravest, the very bravest, can travel undaunted.
In this dark vale where travail may leave you pale
there's an old wives' tale that angry oaks can assail.
There's an evil breeze
flowing through those trees.

I traveled there as it made my hair stand up on the back of my neck.
For while I tread with certain dread, I'm a total nervous wreck.
I felt the clutch of a wooden touch as I walked betwixt the boughs.
It may sound absurd, but the sounds I heard, made me crease my brows.
It wasn't an owl that horrible howl I heard somewhere nearby.
It was long and foul, so long and foul, a craven creature's cry.
There among the trees I feel to my knees praying "God, please save me now."
But with faith destroyed I could not avoid the terror doubts allow.
I was way too late to predict my fate. It was really sink or swim.
So without a word, with my vision blurred, I ran for life and limb.
There's an evil breeze
flowing through those trees.

In daylight these woods are eerie, in the night time they're downright scary.

You may spot a Leprechaun or Fairy, or something that looks hairy.
You think you're free from harm, no need for alarm.
The truth is quite contrary. It's understood that the very wood comes alive. You must not tary.
It may be best, you may have guessed, to consider things possessed.
If you carry a heavy load while on the forest road, you may want to rest
But if you go there become aware, you may get more than fright.
Watch what you sit upon because the things you lean on may bite.
Keep your feet prepared and fleet while considering retreat.
Before you hear it an evil spirit may consider you a treat
So beware of those trees
There's an evil breeze
flowing through those trees.
Beware! Oh please. Oh please!

Author Notes:
Well just look at those trees. They have faces and grasping arms. I used this picture before in Ancient Angry Oaks, but this is a closer look. This poem is a Tambour.. If one can visualize a parade walking by and the sound of the drums as they march. The poetry is set to mimic the sound and roll of a drum.

Poem 13: The Demon's Hand
(An Octogram)

The Demon's Hand is on the land,
and won't let go.
He knows that we don't understand.
So things that grow
are in his grasp, 'cause we forgot
our roles to not let planet rot.
He's moving in to run the show,
and won't let go.

The Demon's Hand is taking Earth,
and soon we'll know
too late, to not ignore its worth.
For long ago,
He promised he would capture it,
if humans failed to keep it fit.
He's got control, to our great woe,
and won't let go.

Author Notes:

So beware! If we don't take care of our planet, Satan will take it over. The signs are already there. I saw this tree and it reminded me of a deformed hand reaching out of the ground to grasp it. That became the inspiration for this poem. So it is an Ekphrastic poem.

This poem is an Ekphrastic Octogram

Ekphrastic is a poem that is written based on the attached image. So, the image came first and was the inspiration.

The Octogram is a style of poetry invented by Sally Yocom (S.Yocom). It consists of two stanzas of eight lines each, with a very specific syllable count and rhyme scheme.
Syllable count is 84848884, repeat on second stanza.
Rhyme scheme: aBabccbB ababddbB, where B repeats same text.
No more than 16 lines.
The tempo is tetrameter on the 8 count line, and dimeter on the 4 count line, but not necessarily iambic.

Poem 14: Possessed
(Rispetto)

In deep dark forest Horrors dwell
Wild beasts, cruel traps, or far, far worse.
Danger lurks in every hidden knell
Where even trees have the Devil's curse

From rotted trunks tendrils immerse
Roots that probe the Earth's very shell
Deeply, to the very Gates of Hell
For angry demons to gain traverse

AH HA HA HA Ha Haaaaaaaaa!

Author Notes:

Faces emerge. The roots go deep into the earth. How far do they go?
This is a photograph I took on Harriet Island near St. Paul, Mn. It struck me as having a dozen evil, smirking faces coming out of the trunk, as if it was possessed. The demons were trying to break free. It inspired me to write this poem. How many faces do you see?

This poem is a Rispetto
A Rispetto, an Italian form of poetry, is a complete poem of two rhymed quatrains with strict meter. The key aspect of a Rispetto involves the rhyme scheme that begins with the standard rhyme in the first stanza, then changes to another in the second. The meter is usually iambic tetrameter with a rhyme scheme of:
abab ccdd.

Chapter 4: Historical Artifacts

I may have stumbled across some items that are mentioned in history.For example, I think I've found a dragon's head washed up on the beach. My gosh, I thought they were only a myth, but there it is. See for yourself.

Aren't Sabertooth Tigers extinct? Then what is one doing in a Lego store?

There are legends that giants once roamed the earth. Possibly before the Flood of Noah. I think I found one half buried.

Native Americans are famous for dancing around a fire, and I spotted one frozen in time.

See it all for yourself.

Poem 15: Dragon's Head
(A Sestet)

What residue lay on this shore?
What remnant shard of ancient lore?
I can't believe what's from the tide,
So evidently petrified.
Its presence there can't be denied,
Although I've never seen it there before.

You may perceive just jetsam junk,
Or driftwood from a rotted trunk,
But scientists will see the eye,
And wood, where bones decalcify,
A rakish ridge with horns nearby,
And even spots where scales were countersunk.

I've read about them in a book,
Foreboding creatures time forsook.
Has it lain hidden in the snow?
This head from myths of long ago,
Through only legends do we know?
Yet evidence here seen can't be mistook.

It surely is a Dragon's head,
Once severed and completely dead.
Did mighty sword from heaven's forge,
In noble hands of good St. George,
Behead this beast to now disgorge
Like refuse on this beach, just steps ahead?

Author Notes:

This is an Animated Still of a driftwood tree trunk that reminds me of a Dragon's skull. I came across it along the Mississippi River. Dragon's bring to mind the legend of St. George. Since George is my middle name, So, I thought I'd share some of his story here. Given the Syrian refugee crisis, I thought a story about a Syrian Christian martyr appropriate.

Saint George (AD 275 to303), was a soldier in the Roman army who later became venerated as a martyr. His father, Gerontius, was a Roman army official and his mother, Polychronia, was a Christian from Lydda in Syria. Saint George became an officer in the Roman army under Emperor Diocletian, who ordered his death for failing to recant his Christian faith. Before that, a dragon makes its nest at the spring for the city of Lydda. The citizens have to dislodge the dragon from its nest to collect water. Each day they offer the dragon a sheep, and if no sheep can be found, a maiden. The victim is chosen by drawing lots. One day, this happens to be the princess. She is offered to the dragon, but then Saint George appears. He faces the dragon, protects himself with the sign of the Cross, slays the dragon, and rescues the princess. The citizens abandon their paganism and convert to Christianity.

This poem is a Sestet.
Sestets are poems with six lines per stanza. They come in many formats. For this one, I use a cadence of :
8,8,8,8,8,10
The rhyme scheme follows the pattern: aabbba in each, but does change the rhyme. It meter is iambic.

Poem 16: Extinct Kitty
(Seastet)

As I rounded the corner, I blinked
At a Cat whose features are Distinct.
So let me be quite Succinct.
I think that Sabertooths are Extinct.
So wouldn't it be a pity
To be pounced on by THIS Kitty?

Author Notes:

Although this doesn't specifically meet the definition of a "face in the clouds, it is such a spectacular assembly of Legosthat I included it here. It certainly is a very animates still life object. I took this picture at LEGO Land in Mall of America, Bloomington, Minnesota. That place is Amazing.

This poem is a Sestet
A Sestet is simply a poem with stanzas that have six lines.

Poem 17: Slumber of the Colossus
(Octaves)

Slumber Deep! Slumber Well!

I wonder what the Eons Tell.
While you slept the World moved on,
Dust and sand to rest your heavy head upon.
While you dreamt, there grew a flower bed,
That centuries since have long fallen dead
As you calmly slept, silent snowflakes fell.
Rain fell, too many times, for the Bards to tell.
Did you Freeze here? or, Are you really dead?

How long has it been since you awoke?
Or walked, or ate, or even spoke?
Were you here when Noah's water rose?
Or when the Glaciers ruled in icy flows?
Did Aztecs offer you bloody sacrifice,
Tossing innocent babes off a high precipice?
Did Mammoths crush you with their mangy toes?
Did you witness Christ when to bread was broke?

I do not hear those slumber sounds!
You must have weighed a million pounds!
So hard to measure that massive girth,
When so much is buried down in the Earth.
You must have grown to 10 feet tall!
Have you broken things when you took a fall,
And left a furrowed field of mighty mounds?
Did you cry out? or feel nothing at all?

Now you lie there in that sweet repose,
With buried chin and crumpled nose.
How many fevered feet have trampled through,
Before Mother Earth has come and buried you?
You lie there, a giant in such silent sleep,
Such ancient secrets still buried deep
As more millennium have marched on by,
We don't know the How, When, or Why.

Author Notes:

Broken Idol? or Colossal statue?
This photograph is one I took in the front yard of a house along Lower Afton Road in St. Paul, Minnesota. I saw a face in the stone decorating the driveway. The whole shot reminded me of a broken giant statue head of a god from ancient times with other pieces strewn about.

This Poem is done in Octaves.
This format is written in 8 Line stanzas, with several choices of meter and rhyme.

Poem 18: Sun Dance

(A Totem Poem)

I
Celebrate
The rising of the sun in the sky.
Then pay tribute to the four winds,
Ki
Yii,
Ki
Yii.
Dance
Like the eagle soaring high,
Entranced by the rhythm of the drum,
Ta
Dum,
Ta
Dum.
So

Ho,
I
Go.
So
Ho.
Ta
Dum,
Ta
Dum.
My feet
On Mother Earth
Pound the rhythms of New Birth,
As I celebrate the rising of the sun.

Author Notes:

I have great respect for Native American Culture. I took this picture of a tree stump in Blue Earth, Minnesota. I t sure looks like a dancing Indian. They celebrate the rising of the sun with respect and joy. I tried to capture both the sound of their incantations as well as the beat of the drums.

This is a Totem Poem. The verse is somewhat shaped like a totem Pole.

Chapter 5: Intriguing Observations

These are things that you look at a maybe do a double take, or just say, "Hmmm, did I really see that?"
Sometimes you may just get that uneasy feeling that you are being watched.

Are there hidden giants watching us (the Watchers)?
Do spirits dance in enchanted forests?
Are there unknown guardians protecting sacred areas?
Can a tree spell?

These are questions that just may be answered in the next chapter. So keep looking over your shoulder. Just maybe you are being watched.

Poem 19: Being Watched
(A Symmetrina Poem)

With darkness drawing near the shadow's
fears recalled
what Giants roamed these woods in days
gone by.
I felt like I was being watched!
My senses burned, felt tracked by evil eye,
all while my racing heart was stalled, my
skin soon crawled.

For there, beyond the turn, was spied large
lurking form.
It seemed to be alive, like vigil guard.
I felt like I was being watched,
by something much too large to disregard
–
this shaded silent presence, far beyond the
norm.

Most disconcerting here, was shape's
enormous size –
a house-size helmet, shading eyes
widespread.
I felt like I was being watched,
by something like Goliath's severed head.
 The eyeballs blinked, to my most mortified
surprise.

Was rendered witless by this object on the
ground.
The Book of Enoch said some "Watchers"
came.
 I felt like I was being watched!
This silent giant, possibly the same,
just may be ancient angel that is still
around.

I felt like I was being watched!

Author Notes:

I hope that you see the image here of a
rock that looks to me like a helmeted head.
If you see the eye sockets, then you can
make out the nose and bearded face
peeking over a berm. What looks like a
shining eye is actually just a weed bending
in front of the stone. I blended in the Story
of the Watchers and Goliath. Besides the
Book of Enoch, the Watchers are
mentioned in the Bible story of Noah. Many
ancient cultures mention the giants that
once existed.

This poem is a Symmetrina.
The Symmetrina was created by
Fanstorian Pantygynt. It is called a
Symmetrina because it presents a
symmetrical shape and rhyme scheme
over each stanza: The rhyme scheme for
each is:
abcba.
The rhythm is iambic throughout. It is
structured in Quintets, which are stanzas
with 5 lines. The first and last lines are
Alexandrine Hexameters (12 syllables), the
second and fourth pentameters (10
syllables) and the third is a tetrameter (8
syllables). So the meter becomes:
12,10,8,10,12.
Note how the rhyme scheme rises (a,b,c),
then falls, while the meter falls (12,10,8),
then rises.
No limit to the number of stanzas.

For this poem I modified the rhyme
scheme a bit. I used the middle unrhymed
line "c" in the middle of the stanza as an
interlinked, repeating line in every stanza. I
also used the "c" line as the closing envoy
to give a somewhat unique overall rhyme
scheme that looks like this:
abCba - deCed - fgCgf - hiCih - C.

Poem 20: Meadow Masquerade
(ABAB Quatrains)

When you think of a typical forest,
and its woodlands, and rivers, and hills,
do they dance and resound in a chorus?
Do they tap to the tune of foothills?

Well I once found a magical meadow,
with the trees and the brush on parade!
All the birds, and the squirrels, in the shadows,
were engaged in a gay masquerade.

In the forest the wildlife were dancing
to the breezes that blew merry tunes.
The warm air was soon full of romancing.
Branches swayed to the sounds of the loon.

When the music pulsates through the jackpine,
all the elves then perform happy tasks,
like each serving up goblets of sweet wine.
There were even tall trees wearing masks.

Even tall trees wearing masks!

Author Notes:

How's that for a poem to accompany this image for my Animated Stills collection? To me, this looks just like a mask on a tree. Maybe it's a stretch, but enough for me to inspire this poem about a masquerade. I thought I'd turn this dreary image into something joyous and active. 2It hope you come away with a festive feeling.

Please note that here, I pronounce the word "Squirrel" in the Americanized vernacular as being a 1 syllable word as in "skewrl."

This poem is simply a set of abab rhymed quatrains. I added a one line envoy to reinforce the subject of my image. It is written in anapestic meter. To me, this anapestic meter is like waltz, rather than the march of iambic meter. It is a more graceful - da da dum da da dum da da dum, as opposed to the other's da dum da dum da dum.
For this poem I used interposed feminine and masculine rhymes, giving a syllable count of 10-9-10-9.

Poem 21: Petrified Warrior
(A Duodecatain Poem)

Petrified warrior, turned to wood,
who died erect, right where he stood,
is silent, deep in forest grave.
What does he see?
What does he hear?
Beyond that tree
 is there a deer?
Does danger travel to his ear,
or is he watching you and me?

This guardian in wilderness,
what power could this thing possess?
Could spirit strength still lie within?
I feel a force in its stone skin.
How did he die?
Can he survive?
Is he a spy?
Is wood alive?
When such an object may revive,
this eerie feel, I can't deny,

This trip is done!
I'll run, run, RUN!

Author Notes:

While out in the woods, I spotted a broken tree that seemed to have a head on its remaining trunk, so I captured its image. I could make out the light outline of an arm, and my imagination also perceived an animal pelt draped across its shoulder. Ah, I thought, here is a warrior or shaman, frozen in time.

This poem is a Duodecatain.
A Duodecatain, a format of my own creation. A decatain is a stanza of ten lines. This format has two, thus the "duo" designation. Here are the rules:
1. The meter is either iambic or trochaic, or a mixture of both.
2. There are two 10 line stanzas followed by a rhyming couplet.
3. The lines are a mix of tetrameter and dimeter with the following syllable counts:
8888444488 8888444488 44
4. The rhyme scheme in each decatain is: aabbcdcddc (but the rhymes can vary between the stanzas).
5. The couplet rhyme is ee. Note that I used questions in this poem, but that is not a requirement.

Poem 22: Spelling Tree
(ABCB Quatrains in Dimeter)

I never knew
A tree could spell,
But here's the tale
That I can tell.

When I was out,
Just passing through,
I saw one form
A "W."

I'm not sure what
It meant to say.
Maybe it meant
To say, "This Way."

Or, maybe it
Was doing best
To show the way
Of going West.

I'm sure that it
Was meaning well.
I never knew
A tree could spell.

Author Notes:

I go by this tree often. It always leaves an impression. The tree branch certainly looks like a W to me. Do my eyes deceive me? What does it mean? It inspired this poem.

This poem is ABCB Quatrains,
These are poems with a standard 4 line stanza (Quatrain) with a rhyme scheme of abcb (skipping), where the first and third line do not rhyme, but the second and fourth do. I wrote it in iambic Dimeter with that abcb rhyme scheme.

Poem 23: Stony Gaze
(A Spenserian Sonnet)

An angry spirit lingers in the rock
Imprisoned there since long forgotten time.
To some it seems a simple sandstone
block
That's coated with some centuries of
grime,
A guardian where people often climb.
Although the effort's difficult and steep,
Because the views up there are so
sublime,
You share them with the likes of Bighorn
Sheep.
Beware! As there are secrets those stones
keep.
You're being watched by wizard's evil eye,
With stare, whose glare may make your
neck skin creep?
It's said that spirit has caused some to die.
    So, if you don't respect that sacred
ground,
    It may be, you'll no longer be
around.

Author Notes:

This is a sandstone outcrop on a cliff know as Dayton's Bluff near downtown St. Paul, Minnesota. I saw in it a very distinguishable eye, a large upturned nose, and somewhat of a face.

The Spenserian sonnet, was invented by Edmund Here, the "abab" pattern sets up distinct four-line groups, each of which develops a specific idea; however, the overlapping a, b, c, and d rhymes form the first 12 lines into a single unit with a separated final couplet. The three quatrains then develop three distinct, but closely related ideas, with a different idea (or commentary) in the couplet. Spenser often begins L9 of his Sonnets with "But" or "Yet," indicating a volta, exactly where it would occur in the Italian Sonnet; however, one often finds that the "turn" here really isn't one at all, that the actual turn occurs where the rhyme pattern changes, with the couplet, thus giving a 12 and 2 line pattern very different from the Italian 8 and 6 line pattern. A Spenserian sonnet does not appear to require that the initial octave set up a problem that the closing sestet answers, as with a Petrarchan sonnet. Instead, the form is treated as three quatrains connected by the interlocking rhyme scheme and closed by a couplet. The linked rhymes of his quatrains suggest the linked rhymes of such Italian forms as terza rima.

Poem 24: Woodland Watcher
(Mixed Formats)

Little woodland sprite
is watching both day and night
security's tight

--<<->>--

What watched in the woods,
from fields of this land,
dismissed where it stood,
stump silently stands,
feet fixed in sand.

Its bark doesn't bite.
Might be surprised,
you'll be in sight
of bulging eyes.

To obey
Nature's way
many say,

when spied
outside,

hide.

--<<->>--

This spirit of tree
Can't easily flee.
When safety applies,
It closes its eyes.

Author Notes

Nature often comes up with some interesting shapes. Like this tree stump I spotted, in Blue Mounds State Park of Southwestern Minnesota, that looks like a little tree creature with bulging eyes. Naturally it tickled my Muse with the following result.

This poem has Mixed Formats
It is comprised of 3 distinct poetic formats: a 5-7-5, a Diminishing Hexaverse, and a closing ABAB Rhymed Quatrain used as an envoi.

A 5-7-5 Poem is simple a poem where line one has 5 syllables, line two has 7 syllables, and line three has 5 syllables again. It need not rhyme, but I chose to mono-rhyme it.

A Diminishing Hexaverse is a poem that begins with a five-line stanza of five syllables in each line, then a four-line stanza with four syllables each, and so on, until the last one syllable stanza ends the poem. The reducing line and syllable count is why the form is referred to as "diminishing." The term "Hexaverse" does not refer to syllable count as much as it does with a "Hex" or "spell" that causes the syllables to disappear with each new stanza. Thus, "poof" it's gone.

ABAB Rhymed Quatrain.
I chose a tight 5 syllable count Quatrain (4 lined stanza) with an abab rhyming scheme to close the poem.

Chapter 6: Mythical Magical

In this chapter we find things that are either mythical or magical. Remember in Walt Disney's movie Fantasia, that Mickey Mouse got broom sticks to do his chores, but it got out of control?
How about trees walking? How about a pride of lions being frozen in place like a group of Sphinxes?
Or, three witches getting their brooms? Magical indeed.

The Phoenix bird rose from the ashes to become a Firebird in mythology. Did we see one before our eyes?

Another myth is an Abominable Snowman. There are also stories of giant snowbirds. Could one be lurking during winter on the shores of Lake Superior?

I guess we'll just have to see. Turn the page.

Poem 25: Enchanted Forest
(Tercets)

You might think this Dumb
Enchanted Trees move on for Some
Call them they will Come

Author Notes:

As I stood on the beach along the Mississippi River bank and looked up, I got the strangest impression that the woods was creeping on its roots down to the river. Like Mickey Mouse's enchanted brooms in Walt Disney's movie Fantasia, these trees seemed to have come alive and are walking. My imagination? Maybe.

This poem is a Tercet
Tercets are simply poems with 3 line stanzas. This one is also a special subcategory called a 5-7-5, as it is also holds a syllabic formula. Line 1 is 5 syllables. Line 2 is 7. Finally, line 3 reverts to 5 syllables. Thus the designation.

Poem 26: Firebird
(A Sonnet)

Oh Firebird, of myth and ash,
Your purpled plumes rise from the
flames,
And like the heat returning sun,
Renewal forms your mythic claims.

Oh Phoenix, formed from fire's force,
Your legend burns across the sky,
In trails of smoke and glowing arch,
On toasted wings that make sparks fly.

Oh Benu glyph of ancient myth,
In resurrection of the soul,
Set free the purgatory lost
Their spirit cleanse to make them whole.

And once their essence has renewed
Feed them with your spiritual food

Author Notes

This poem is about rebirth, resurrection, renewal as symbolized by the Firebird of myth and legend that is known in many cultures. Known to the Native Americans as the Firebird, interestingly enough, that's also what the Russians called it. Of course many believe Native Americans came across the frozen Bearing Straights, after the last ice age ended, from Mongolia. The Ancient Greeks had their legend of the Phoenix. Ancient Egypt had a similar legend of the Benu. Also associated with the color purple, considered royal in nature. Due to its characteristic of resurrection, early Christians adopted it as symbol for Jesus Christ. There are other examples in other cultures. The Persians had the Anka; Turkish had Kerkes, Tibetians had the Me byi karmo, and the Chinese had the Fenghuang. I tried to blend these mythologies into the poem.

Purgatory is believed to be a place between Heaven and Hell, where blemished souls, await their cleansing, to be allowed into Heaven. Some believe that Christ released them upon His death and resurrection.

This poem is a Sonnet, written in iambic tetrameter using the abcb rhyme scheme.

This picture is a gnarled tree stump in Blue Mounds State Park of Southwestern Minnesota. It reminded me of a bird sitting on a perch in the foreground (look for a wing) ready to fly out of the smoke that is billowing and rising up behind it.

Poem 27: Ice Lions
(Dandizette)

The frozen lions of the ice,
asleep in Winter's chill,
dream of tropical paradise
while sitting on this frigid hill.
What caused them to be here?
A magic touch of wizard's will?

Their genesis is far from clear.
Unknown, the cause remaining still.
The consequence of doom, I fear.
Their tomb – the ice, upon this shore.
Don't deign to draw too near,
caught in its spell forevermore.

Asleep in Winter's chill,
What caused them to be here?
Unknown, the cause remaining still.
Don't deign to draw too near.
For the wisp of the wind is death,
and the ice may draw your last breath.

Author's notes:

This image captured my imagination, as I see at least 3 lions in it. I hope that you do too. I gave it a sinister interpretation. The poem will become part of my Animated Still collections, which I hope to publish later this year.

This poem is a Dandizette.
The format was sponsored by the FanStory Potlatch Poetry Club this week. So I thought I'd try one. Dandizette form created by Discoveria of Allpoetry.com is composed of 3 six line stanzas. The form is partially inspired by the villanelle and features a tricky repetition of 4 refrain lines in the final stanza.

The form is syllabic with a syllable count for the first two stanzas is:
8/6/8/8/6/8.
The last stanza has lines of:
6/6/6/6/8/8 syllables.
The rhyme scheme is:
a,B1,a,b,C1,b, - c,B2,c,d,C2,d - B1,C1,B2,C2,e,e. (The capital letters designate the repeated lines, while the numbers differentiate them from where they were originally located)
The final stanza is composed of lines 2 (B1), 5 (C1), 8 (B2), and 11 (C2) from the previous two stanzas, plus a concluding rhyming couplet. Where they reappear
in the last stanza, the four repeated lines should
make sense together as well as making sense where they
are first used.
Meter is optional.

Poem 28: Snow Monsters
(Free Verse)

Are snow monsters real
with sharp
crystal teeth
devouring roof tops
in gigantic gulps?

Oh woe!

What to think,

when
the unsuspecting,
all very warm and cozy,
drinking their hot chocolate
and snuggled under thick quilts,

have
their
rafters
come
tumbling
down?

Remember
those
small round
remorseless eyes
that hunger for a tasty treat.

No structure is safe
From the icy fangs.

They'll crunch
Both bed and bones!

Are you safe is your house
from the freezing crush?

Beware!

Author Notes

Snow is eating my roof! Oh what, oh what can I do? I've heard about snow monsters. The most famous of course is the Abominable Snowman, Yeti. Winter is when the snow monsters are born. This one seems to be a giant bird-like creature. This image reminded me of that large bird-like snow monster biting a house roof. Maybe my imagination has run away a bit.

This poem is Free Verse
Free Verse poetry is a very open and free flowing form of poetry written without required formats. There is no fixed meter, tempo, or rhyme. The author, instead, paints a poetic picture with the words. The author adds dimension in how the poem is felt, through the use of pace and pause, created in how the words are arranged on the page. This can create very moving thoughts and images. Done correctly, it can turn simple sentences into lovely works of art.

Poem 29: Writhing Wraiths
(ABCedarian)

After dark on Summer's Eve they sashay,
Beneath the silver shade at river's edge.
Cavorting, dancing, prancing hand in hand
Dancing were Witches of the meadow glade.
Enchanting – Giselle, Xena, Marilee,
Flowing in circles go the haunting three
Giselle's lilting laughter filling the night
Having a grand, and joyous holiday.
Into the night they danced and pranced, and sang.
Just wistful wraiths whirling the hours away
Keeping the cackling spirit world at bay.
'Lest Lucifer and his fiends come to stay.
Marilee merrily marching, matching beat.
Naughty pulsing, insatiable heat,
Offering their spirits to god Mother
Praying here for the gift to be bequeathed.
Quaking, praying, shaking with a shiver
Rapping with jungle music all around
Surrounded by the eerie night time sounds
To them a question comes from hot thin air
Unspoken but felt deep within their souls
Very close, it whispered on the wind,
"What would writhing Witches want?" the god said.
Xena replied "Oh! Just to fly away."
Yes! The Queen of Nature released the spell.
Zoom! On Brooms, the grass witches flew away.

Author Notes:

A witches Tale in alphabet. Three Young Witches get their wings, so to speak. Here I introduce them for the first time: Giselle, Xena, and Marilee. These three may show further in my work.

This Poem is based on this photograph I took in February along the Mississippi River bank at Hidden Falls in Minnesota. When I first saw the image, I thought it reminded me of forest spirits, Wraiths if you will, dancing in the forest.

This poem is an ABCedarian
An ABCedarian poem is one using the 26 letters of the alphabet chronologically. It is a special form of an Acrostic poem in which the initial letters of the words that begin each line of the poem, or stanza, spell out the alphabet, in order. No meter required. Rhyming optional.

Chapter 7: Religious

Here we have, some poems that have a religious tone to them, inspired by the image shown. We can't hide our sins. God sees everything, even those.

As cultures developed, religion became the source of much good, but also of much evil. I see the interplay of religion as a root of culture.

God left traces of His handiwork throughout the world, and I've found one here. When Moses died, legend has it that God kissed him.

All this unfolds before us in this chapter.

Poem 30: God's Eye
(A Villanelle)

The Eye of God is looking down,
Sometimes with joy, most times with
pain.
Our sins toward Him may make it frown.

Unfaithful souls, in sin we drown,
Without a thought what wrath we gain.
The Eye of God is looking down.

An evil cloaked gossamer gown
Can't fool His Eye, the taints remain.
Our sins toward Him may make it frown.

For Satan is a lying clown
Who bends the truth of his distain.
The Eye of God is looking down.

In heaven see God's golden crown.
His Eye sees what our hearts contain.
Our sins toward Him may make it frown.

Beware delights demons explain.
They deal confusion to our brain.
The Eye of God is looking down.
Our sins toward Him may make it frown.

Author Notes:

A couple of nights ago I captured a sunset. Within it was this image. It made me think of an angry eye in the sky and became the inspiration for this poem. I also must thank fellow FanStorian, tfawcus. Tony reminded me of this lovely format that I hadn't written in a while.

This poem is a Villanelle.
A villanelle is a nineteen-line poetic form consisting of five tercets followed by a quatrain. There are two refrains (A1 and A2) and two repeating rhymes (a and b), with the first and third line of the first tercet repeated alternately until the last stanza, which includes both repeated lines. The villanelle is an example of a fixed verse form. It is structured by two repeating rhymes and two refrains: the first line of the first stanza serves as the last line of the second and fourth stanzas, and the third line of the first stanza serves as the last line of the third and fifth stanzas.

The rhyme-and-refrain pattern of the villanelle can be schematized as:
(A1)b(A2) ab(A1) ab(A2) ab(A1) ab(A2) ab(A1)(A2)
where letters ("a" and "b") indicate the two rhyme sounds, upper case indicates a repeated refrain ("A"), and superscript numerals (1 and 2) indicate Refrain A1 and Refrain A2.
There is no specific meter required for a Villanelle, but for this poem I chose iambic tetrameter.

This photograph was taken at dusk by the author on Saturday, April 4, 2015. Interestingly, that is the day after Good Friday, and a day before Easter Sunday.

Poem 31: The Root and Religion
(Etherees)

Our ancient ancestors sought to reveal
Many mysteries of the Universe
To see the star's magical clues
Answers from the Cosmos
Left undone as they
Seek far and wide
To find the
Primal

Root

Of all
So very deep
Within Religion
The Foundation stone
To build vast settlements
And awesome structures of stone
Finally Mankind evolved organization
With complex socially structured rules
The Formation of Civilization

Religion

Blind Faith, Devotion, Total Sacrifice
Double-edged Sword leads to Hate and
War
Purges, Pogroms, and Holocaust
Crucifixions and Crusades
Holiest Rites Unyielding
Aloft Burning Cross
Witch at the Stake
The Good and
Evil

Root

Author Notes:

The Seeds of Civilization are in the ultimate religions that they support. All major civilizations throughout history centered their societies around the foundations of their Religion whether Egypt, Rome, Greece, Aztec Central America, Mayan South America, Isreal, China, or India. They were all structured by their belief systems. Some are for better some for worse

This image is taken of a large root at Harriet Island. In the background is the Cathedral of St. Paul.

This poem is made of of Etherees. In fact, a suite of Tumbling Ethreees
An Etheree is a syllabic format, intended to make a pleasing shape. Therefore, careful attention should be given to the size of the words, so that the outline of the poem forms as straight a line as possible. Jagged edges are not acceptable.
An Etheree has 10 lines with a syllable count of:
1-2-3-4-5-6-7-8-9-10.
When double, the next stanza's syllable count is reversed to:
10-9-8-7-6-5-4-3-2-1.
There is no requirement to rhyme, but a poet can choose to do so.

A tumbling Etheree alternates between the original form, and a reversed one.

Poem 32: Rose Within a Stone
(Octaves)

A Great Designer touched this very rock,
Whose fingers chiseled patterns in the stone,
Way long before the concept of a clock,
Or even prior to a living bone.
This pattern spotted, caused a major shock,
Perceiving it was wrought by God alone.
For who but He could carve on granite block,
Then leave it here on Earth for us to own,

A rose within a stone.

His laser touch was seen just once before.
On hard slate tablets Heaven's words were hewn.
When Moses brought Commandments to the fore.
But he returned from mountain top too soon,
In anger, broke them all on valley's floor,
Then God replaced his words, next afternoon,
And hid them 'hind the tabernacle door.
Yet this stone's just as magic as a rune,

A rose within a stone.

For this is still a very special place.
A place where God's good work is everywhere.
He must have drawn some plans within this space.
The evidence is scattered here and there.
The work of His creation's left a trace,
Of little sketches meant to help compare
From which new pretty pattern to embrace.
To find a blueprint, still, is very rare,

A rose within a stone.

Author Notes:

If you look at the top of this rock, there is an indentation that looks like the flower of a Rose. I hope you can see it. If you do, you might also see the hint of a stem, maybe even some petals. This is the image that inspired my poem to go on a flight of fancy.

The rock is located in the Japenese Garden at Como Park, St. Paul, Minnesota. If you go there. Look for it.

This poem is written in Octaves, or Octrains (8 Lines stanzas), with a repeated refrain. The rhyme scheme uses alternating rhymes, or: abababab R. Except for the refrains, the meter is iambic pentameter.

Poem 33: The Kiss of God
(Ballad)

The Torah tells of Moses' death
with "Al pi Adonai."
As he was breathing his last breath,
God kissed him from on high.

He never touched the Promised Land,
still he was dearly loved.
For there upon the Sinai sand,
God kissed him from above.

Observers are all awed.
The angels all applaud,
the Kiss of God.

Imagine the clouds gathering,
as scarlet face protrudes
from purple nimbus, capturing
a Godly attitude.

The regal cloud then hovers low
containing loving lips
that reached down to the man below,
emotions to eclipse.

Observers are all awed.
The angels all applaud,
the Kiss of God.

This was a noted incident,
when God was in this state,
but not the only precedent
receiving Godly fate.

God often kisses things He loves,
those things of greatest worth.
His way of showing He approves.
He even kisses Earth!

Observers are all awed.
The angels all applaud,
the Kiss of God.

Author Notes:

The sky was awesome the other day, and I took a picture of it with my cell phone from a parking lot. In looking at it later, I noticed, just to the left of center, what looked like lips. Above them you can make out the semblance of a nose and eyes - a face in the sky! I said to myself -"This would make a wonderful Animated Still." But I needed a Muse. So I searched the internet for a story about a face in the sky, and was delighted to come across the story of Moses.

Here's how The Talmud describes it. In a Blog by Rabbi Brant Rosen, I read: "Readers of the Torah often comment on the seeming unfairness of God's decree that Moses must die before he can enter the Promised Land. But when we reach the final verses of the Torah, the tone feels anything but untimely or tragic. Rather, God's treatment of Moses in his final moments hints at a spirit of love and tenderness."
"Commentators have made much of the words "al pi adonai - "at the command of the Lord," which literally means "at the mouth of the Lord." In the midrashic imagination, this verse is commonly read: "Moses died-at the kiss of God." Some have pointed out the poignant symmetry of this image: just as God breathes life into the first human, God reclaims Moses' soul through a similar loving act."
I tried to capture the gist of of that story, while accommodating my image as well. I also blended in the thought of a similar love for the Earth. God's kiss as rain.

This poem is a simple Ballad, using the signature 8-6 tempo, an abab rhyme scheme, and a 3 line repeated chorus, having a 6,6,4 mono-rhymed meter.

Chapter 8: Revealed Mystery

This group most likely will be the most difficult, because you'll have to look closely to see the image that is hidden within. This section takes the most imagination to detect. But I hope that makes it more rewarding. Whether you see alien, demonic, ghostly, elfin, snow, or smoky forms depends on you.

Whether you do or not see what I do, I hope you enjoy the poem. But I think most of you will. I do give you hints in the poem's notes.

Poem 34: Alien Skull
(A Whitney)

In a tree,

alien skull.

Secret eyes

are fairly dull.

Hard to spot

this hidden hull.

Why was it left there to rot?

Author Notes:

Using a bit of imagination, I see an alien skull here. It's not a solid skull by any means, but a rotted remnant hung on a tree to dangle like a bangle. You'll have to look hard for the eye sockets, then it comes together with a straight line mouth at the bottom.

This poem is a Whitney.

The Whitney poem format was created by Betty Ann Whitney. This is a seven-line versed poem based on Japanese patterns with a fixed syllable format that contains

3, 4, 3, 4, 3, 4, 7 syllables respectively.

No rhyme scheme is required, but may be incorporated if desired. For this poem I did use a rhyme scheme. It is:

ababcbc.

This photograph was taken by the author himself, of a snowy tree branch in his back yard.

Poem 35: Elfin King

(ABAB Quatrains)

Spirit of the summer flowers,
Hidden there in the brightest blooms,
Elfin King with mystic powers
Concealed in camouflage costume.

I see your impish beaming grin.
Your eyes and beard give you away.
What secrets do you hide within
That colorful arranged bouquet?

Knowing you can grant some wishes,
And I've caught you hiding there,
Will you deign to grant some riches,
Or disappear into thin air?

Author Notes:

The little spirits hide in plain sight. Even in flower arrangements, where they blend right in. Look closely and you'll spot them. Find this little guy at the white flower in the lower left corner.

This poem is ABAB Quatrains.
These are poems with a standard 4 line stanza (Quatrain) with a rhyme scheme of abab (alternating).

I wrote these ABAB rhymed quatrains on a mixed 8 syllable meter.

Poem 36: The Ghost Fish
(An Octogram)

A fish appeared from arctic blue,
just like a ghost.
A phantom you could see right through!
I was engrossed
in this opaque new mystery,
without a well-known history.
Its presence seemed surreal, almost.
Just like a ghost.

I thought I'd try to capture it,
at my utmost.
Alas, the fish did not permit
a single dose
of any human interaction.
Creating stymied satisfaction,
by disappearing undermost.
Just like a ghost.

Author Notes:

You never know what might appear through a crack in the ice. I expected to maybe see a fish, but not one you see right through. This is just some ice in a stream, but I thought it looked like a fish head in the lower left. I spotted it along Battle Creek in St. Paul, Minnesota.

This poem is an Octogram.
The Octogram is a style of poetry invented by Fanstorian Sally Yocom (S.Yocom). It consists of two stanzas of eight lines each, with a very specific syllable count and rhyme scheme.

Syllable count is: 84848884, repeat on second stanza.

Rhyme scheme: aBabccbB ababddbB, where B repeats same text. No more than 16 lines. Strict iambic meter on all lines.

Poem 37: Ghostly Winter Ball
(Rondseau)

The Ghostly choir sings, while gathered at the falls,
Seeking resonance like at the symphony halls,
Drawn by the merry music of the water's sound.
A waterfall's clear tone is Nature's best around,
When eerie haunted tunes echo off frozen walls.

They gathered there to practice for their fancy Balls.
Soon phantom sounds are followed by their spooky calls,
While lady fairies gaily dance around the mound,
The Ghostly choir sings.

Wild water really dances while the chorus drawls
To hip hop melody the mad maestro installs.
Just can't stop twinkling toes from tapping on the ground.
Chances advance as spirited devil's play abound.
Moonglow shines brightly, as a magic mood recalls,
The Ghostly choir sings

Author Notes:

It's said that on a cold winter evening, about dusk and beyond, you can hear an eerie tune at a frozen Minnehaha Falls Maybe it's just the rushing water through long icicles acting like pipe organs, but if you look closely, you can also see a choir of ghosts. I have. Here's the proof.

This poem is a Rondeau. A Rondeau is a fixed form of poetry. It is often used in light or witty poems. It often has fifteen octo - or decasyllabic lines with three stanzas. It usually only has two rhymes (a & b) used in the poem. A word or words from the first part of the first line are used as a refrain ending the second and third stanzas. The rhyme scheme, then, is;

aabba aabR aabbaR.

The format can carry any type of meter or syllable count, as long as it follows the fixed pattern.

Poem 38: My Forest Friend
(A Retourne Poem)

What creatures hide betwixt the wood,
Doth lurk in hidden crooks of trees?
Strange looks make them misunderstood -
Their gentle personalities.

Doth lurk in hidden crooks of trees,
Too shy to make true presence known,
There're few more bashful sprites than
these.
Quite frequently they're all alone.

Strange looks make them misunderstood.
'Tis due to their misshapen head,
Whose eyes portray death's likelihood,
And howling maw, cause fear and dred.

Their gentle personalities,
Beknown to me, I shall defend,
And offer friendly dignities,
When e'er I spot my forest friend.

Author Notes:

I like to spot things that look strange and create a story poem about them. This is just a broken tree limb in the forest, but I see a spooky looking face of a howling forest spirit. So, it inspired this poem
This poem is formatted as a Retourne.

The Retourne poem is another French poem style. Like the Quatern, the Retourne poem has four quatrains (four-line stanzas), and each line has eight syllables. Also, like the Quatern, the Retourne poem does not have to rhyme.
The Retourne poem uses the second, third, and fourth lines of the first stanza as Refrain lines for the first line of the following three stanzas: line two of the first stanza becomes line one of the second stanza, line three becomes line one of the third stanza, and line four becomes line one of the fourth (and last) stanza.
Even though they do not have to rhyme or follow a specific meter, I have chosen to write this Retourne poem in iambic tetrameter with a rhyme scheme of:
a1,B1,A2,B2 B1,c,b,c A2,d,a,d B2,e,b,e
where the first and third lines of each stanza rhyme and where the second and fourth lines of each stanza rhyme, and B1,A2,and B2 represent the Refrains from the first lines in the poem.

This photograph was taken by the author in the woods at Maplewood Preserve in St. Paul, Minnesota.

Poem 39: Sacred Snowbird of Superior

(Free Verse

Giant snowbird!

Come take
a
deep
refreshing drink

Slack your thirst
in the cool clear waters
of
Lake Superior

Sacred Snowbird
white as winter
wings of solid snow
Dip
your beak

Drink deep

Too soon
you will be
gone

Disappearing
into the silence

Dripping
as you drink

What
Will become of you?

Author Notes:

Ice on Lake Superior forms unusual shapes that stimulate the imagination. This one appears to be a large bird, there for those who see. Flying low and surfing the waves,
it's there for only a season. A Metaphor for winter. Author's Photograph taken on the North Shore of Lake Superior.

Lack of punctuation Intended by Author

This poem is Free Verse.
Free Verse poetry is a very open and free flowing form of poetry written without required formats. There is no fixed meter, tempo, or rhyme. The author, instead, paints a poetic picture with the words. The author adds dimension in how the poem is felt, through the use of pace and pause, created in how the words are arranged on the page. This can create very moving thoughts and images. Done correctly, it can turn simple sentences into lovely works of art.

Poem 40: The Eyes on Me
(English Sonnet)

These chilly canyons hide strange
companions, to my surprise.
I hear the cackle hidden in the crackle of
the ice,
And I despise that feel of eyes my senses
realize.
The ghosts are there, must be somewhere,
I felt it once or twice.

Behind each boulder, eyes upon my
shoulder, are so vague.
But will he show, this man of snow, whose
hidden in the wall?
It seems he blends where ice suspends
from every little crag.
What I can't see I want to flee. I don't like
this at all!

Oh! There he is, that mug of his, I see him
hiding there.
His hollow eyes can't be disguised, so
large they point him out.
That toothless mouth was facing south. I
really didn't care
To see him there, up in the air, just
hanging all about.

Now I see other ghosts among those
frozen posts, but you,
Whose voice annoys with creepy noise,
come showing through.

Author Notes:

If you look for a circular eye in the middle
right side of this photograph that I took of a
hanging ice formation, you might see the
toothless face that I'm referring to in this
Animated Still poem. If you have a very
active imagination, you might see some
others. I see a phantom above and to the
left, with a frozen arm pointing downward. I
took that as the direction to the south that I
referred to. Then there is a small head to
the far left. I hope your imagination can
make something out. This photograph was
taken January 23, 2016 at Minnehaha Falls
Park in Minneapolis, Minnesota.

This poem is an English Sonnet.
A traditional English Sonnet is a poem of
14 lines. It follows a strict Rhyme Scheme.
It is often about love, but doesn't have to
be. It consists of 14 lines, each line
containing ten Syllables and is written in
iambic Pentameter, in which a pattern of
an Unstressed Syllable followed by a
Stressed
Syllable is repeated five times. The rhyme
scheme in a English Sonnet is:
a-b-a-b, c-d-c-d, e-f-e-f, g-g.
The last two lines are a Rhyming Couplet.

109

Poem 41: The Face in the falls
(AABB Quatrains)

You may wonder about the Sin
That imprisoned him within
Those mossy granite walls,
The Face within the Falls

You can see his silent moan,
As he struggles here alone
And the echo of his calls
As he emerges from the Falls.

Who is this ancient soul?
What was his fateful role?
His fate remains unknown.
Eternally locked inside the stone.

Author Notes:

An unknown warrior's face is locked eternally within this waterfalls, We wonder how and why. He doesn't seem happy there, and maybe is trying to break out. This image is from a photograph I took of the Cross River Falls on the North Shore of Minnesota. I didn't really notice the face until I downloaded the image onto my IPAD. Actually there is more than one face in this falls, but I was inspired by the large one you should be able to see if you focus on the nose.

This Poem is written in AABB Quatrains. These are poems written in a standard 4 line stanza (Quatrain) with a rhyme scheme of aabb (coupled).

Poem 42: The Heart of the City

(An Alfred Dorn Sonnet)

I traveled down the central city street
in downtown, where the buildings frame
the sky,
where architecture reigns, like mountain
peaks,
and cars roam canyons made from formed
concrete,
as trains and buses often wander by
the buildings bonded using bridge
techniques.

These manmade monuments consume the
scene,
and green's a color seldom ever seen.

And yet, there's beauty often even there!
An ordered chaos sets this sight apart.
Unique details are hidden everywhere,
while ancient often meets state-of-the-art.
Now note that smokey statement in the air
that says that "Even cities have a heart."

Author Notes:

Manmade mountains with cars roaming the canyons is how I see it. The heart in the smoke is a special treat. This is Fourth Street in downtown St. Paul, Minnesota. I wrote this Ekphrastic poem that describes the scene as I observed it from a skywalk while my wife and I enjoyed a winter walk. I was drawn by the smoke, and was amazed to see the some of it formed a heart. That was real, not in any way doctored.

This is an Alfred Dorn Sonnet.
An Alfred Dorn Sonnet is named after its creator and is distinguished by two Sestets bridged by a Couplet. The first one is an Italian Sestet, having a Rhyme Scheme of: abcabc.
The second one is a Sicilian Sestet, taking the Scheme of: aeaeae.
So the entire
Rhyme Scheme becomes:
abcabc dd aeaeae.
Note that the "a" Rhyme is a Linking Rhyme between the 2 Sestets. Written in iambic
Pentameter. The turn (or Volta) is at line 9, as in most Sonnets.

113

Poem 43: The Rushmore Tree
(Mono-rhymed Quintains)

You may think I'm idiotic
Or possibly psychotic.
It was definitely exotic
And slightly Patriotic,
When I found that tree.

I was off to the races
While counting out my paces,
When I came upon the faces
That had left familiar traces,
On the Rushmore tree.

There were only two upon it,
Right along the side. Dog gone it!
As artistic hands had drawn it,
Or a chainsaw dude had sawn it
On that Amazing tree

First was Jefferson's noble chin,
That displayed a friendly grin,
Then his profile was filled in.
His curly hair was held within
That gnarly old tree

If you haven't heard enough, Sir
Believe I'm not a slougher
But Washington was tougher
'Cause the bark around was rougher
On that Rushmore tree

Let your imagination fly!
Just look for the mouth and eye
That is gazing at the sky.
You might see him if you try!
That's the Rushmore tree.

Author Notes:

Now that's what you call Presidential Bark!
A little visual exercise for those who see
with imagination.

I took this photograph of this tree trunk
along the lower path of the Bruce Vento
Trail in what is known as Swede Hollow
just off Downtown St. Paul, MN. What
attracted me were the two unusual knobs
on the tree. I immediately noticed that the
one on the right looked to me like a profile
of Thomas Jefferson. The image of
Washington is not as noticeable, but it
starts with a mouth that looks like it's
holding a cigar butt. That image is what
inspired me to write this little poem.

This poem is written in Quintains, mono-
rhymed.
A Quintain is a poem with stanzas of 5
lines. Also known as a Quintrain, or
a Quintet. It can be a single stanza, or
many. It can be of any meter or rhyme
scheme. Some can be mono-rhymed.

Poem 44: Gogli-eyed Loved
(A Susnika Poem)

What's this as I alight?
Love, gogli-eyed!
Churned up inside
By the fireside.
Maybe romance tonight?

Why am I gogli-eyed?
I'm at a loss,
As my eyes cross,
Then turn and toss.
My love can't be denied!

Author Notes:

Even insects find love. Ok, this guy isn't exactly inanimate, and probably shouldn't be in this collection, but I couldn't' resist capturing those eyes that amused me so. The cross-eyed expression is almost human. I reminded me of a love struck cartoon character. I called the expression "gogli-eyed". This picture is of a dragonfly that I photographed at my campsite at Lake Elmo, Minnesota.

This poem is a Susnika.
A SUSNIKA exploring human emotions. It is a fusion form of Tanka and Nanni poems, just like an Acronet or Quonac but with a twist. A SUSNIKA is a five liner poem like a Tanka and with a 24 syllable count like a nanni, but with a twist (nassus1957 modified version) of the fixed syllable count of Tanka 5/7/5/7/7 into 6/4/4/4/6 syllable count instead. The first and last lines are rhymed but the remaining lines with 4 syllable count are unrhymed, although, I chose to rhyme them.

Chapter 9: Winter

Winter provided some good snow images to inspire these poems. They were taken right around my own house, here in Minnesota, during the winter. Whether sitting or lounging on my back deck, or even in a fissure of ice, winter has an impact that can be seen. So join me in visiting Winter.

Poem 45: Lazy Snow
(Faux Free Style)

You lazy snow
that's lounging on my deck.
Your shape has grown
from just
a crystal speck
to
such a walrus-like
atrocity.

I welcomed you
when
you were itty-bitty.

But now you seem to plan
an overstay.

I hear
more friends will soon be on their way,
and
as you occupy my back yard deck
my house thermometer,
I'll double-check.

For, like a lion,
March came stalking in,
where February's snow's already been
to leave you
lying there in my deck chair.
while growing thick and debonair.

So,
soon there'll be warming sun,
I pray,
to take your chilly friends,
and you,
away.

I'll watch,
as you so slowly
melt and shrink,
and by my window,
sit and sip my drink.

Author Notes

Winter seems so relaxed lounging on my back deck. tIt doesn't seem ready to leave soon either. This visitor appeared during February, 2019, with more snow expected. I measured it at about 2.5 feet in depth so far.

This poem is A Faux Free Style. A Free Style poem is a type of Free Verse with rhyming, usually incidental. What makes this Faux Free Style, is that although I has the look of a Freed Verse poem, it actually has aabb rhyming, as well as iambic pentameter.

121

Poem 46: Muse Served Cold
(A Rispetto)

In frozen drifts of mind I thrive
As thoughts are thawed from crevices
Imagination comes alive
With fissures as apprentices

To blow like snow from Winter's breath
In words that rival Bard's Macbeth
Derived from icy pillars, cold
With phrases blue and written bold

Author Notes:

I see a Gargoyle lurching over the left wall of this artic crevice. There are other leering faces too, if you only have the imagination to see them here in this icy photo. This picture is from a crack in Battle Creek, located in Maplewood Minnesota. Winter provides ample opportunities to observe such wonders. You just need to look. From the Frozen Tundra to your warm eyes.

This poem is a Rispetto
A Rispetto, an Italian form of poetry, is a complete poem of two rhymed quatrains with strict meter. The key aspect of a Rispetto involves the rhyme scheme that begins with the standard rhyme in the first stanza, then changes to another in the second. The meter is usually iambic tetrameter with a rhyme scheme of:
abab ccdd.

Poem 47: Old Man Winter
(ABAB Quatrains)

Old Man Winter came to see me.
He sat upon my deck.
He grabbed a chair auspiciously,
And didn't move a fleck.

He looked so stately sitting there,
Relaxing in my chair,
Reflecting sparkles everywhere
In crispy morning air.

I wondered just how long he'd stay.
What was his wayward mood?
I hadn't seen him yesterday,
When on that deck I stood.

He seemed to want to stay awhile,
Relaxing in the snow,
And watching, I just had to smile.
I knew he wouldn't go.

But then, I got my shovel out.
He didn't seem to fear.
But as I tossed the snow about,
I made him disappear.

Author Notes:

When winter comes to visit, he may stay awhile, A shovel helps. This is another image taken of my back back deck. Another winter from another year. These visitor come and go. I don't really begrudge them. As long as they don't stay too long.

This poem is written in ABAB Quatrains. These are poems with a standard 4 line stanza (Quatrain) with a rhyme scheme of abab (alternating).

Chapter 10: Shocking Discoveries

What are shocking discoveries? They are those items you look at and become frightened, startled, or even possibly afraid. It can also be a sight that makes you say, "Oh my God!" Like when you suddenly see an alligator at your feet, or a large snake dangling right in front of you. If you spotted a bear cub up a tree just above you, you might wonder where its mother is. In a dark woods you could stumble upon a screaming banshee. Those would all give me the chills. How about coming out after a tornado to see the damage that was done?

Yes, those are the things we'll encounter in our journey through this chapter. If you're quick enough to spot them, you heartbeat may start racing. Be ready!

Poem 48: Alligator Allegations
(Septets)

The lizard slithered through the slime,
arising from the mists of time,
to wallow in the iridescent muck.
What, to my unfortunate luck,
did fortune let laboriously climb
just moments from my feet?
I must retreat!

For fear had gripped my very soul,
and from my wits, taken its toll.
But wait! I now perceive, it's just a branch!
From this tree bough, I need not blanch.
My nerves have now regained complete control.
The likenesses' deceit
sent me offbeat.

Author Notes:

Hah! I was out walking along a swamp platform located at the Dodge Nature Center in Mendota Heights, Minnesota, when I came across this object in the water. It sure looked like an alligator. Of course, there are no alligators in Minnesota. It's too cold in the winter for them to survive. So I was a bit surprised, until I realized that it was only a tree branch. I took this picture and wrote this poem.

The Poem is a set of Septets
Septets are poems with 7 line stanzas. Not an established format, that I am aware of. Just something I put together. I was playing a bit with line lengths, so the syllable pattern is:
8,8,10,8,10,6,4 and
8,8,10,8,10,6,4.
The rhyme scheme is:
a,a,b,b,a,c,c d,d,e,e,d,a,a.

129

Poem 49: Hoo Doo 1
(ABAB Quatrains)

Up by the river bank the Hoo Doo Howl,
Their Erie sound Haunting the Forest Height.
You might mistake it for merely an owl
Or a Werewolf stalking the Shadowy Night
In the grasses they hide by the watery path
So consider your course whatever you do
Stay clear of their Haunts, or incur the Wrath,
Of a frightening Forest type Hoo Doo.

Author Notes:

Be Careful Where You Step!
A photograph I took along the Path at Harriet Island in the Mississippi near St. Paul, Minnesota. I had just passed it, looked over my shoulder, and snapped the shot in about two seconds without really thinking about it. When I got home and reviewed the pictures I had taken that day, this image of a howling head really grabbed me.

This poem is written in ABAB Quatrains.
These are poems with a standard 4 line stanza (Quatrain) with a rhyme scheme of abab (alternating).

131

Poem 50: Hoo Doo 2
(Octaves)

Howl Haunting Hoo Doo!
Blow at the Wind like you do.
Piercing Screams that go through
The Night, that Clings like New Dew,
Are the Soulful Songs that draw You
To the Fate that Lies before you.
Banshees, Ghouls, and VooDoo!
Howl away! Howl away dreaded Hoo Doo!

Author Notes:

Of things that go bump in the night. Yes, this image did inspire two different poems. Why a second one? I had originally entered this photograph, with poem, in a contest, but had some problems with it, and I missed the deadline. Since I couldn't enter the same one, I had to write a new poem for it. So, this is the second one. Which one do you like better?

This poem is an Octave This format is written in Octaves, or Octrains (8 Lines stanzas), with several choices of meter and rhyme. For this poem, I chose to completely mono-rhyme it on a mixed meter.

Poem 51: Snake of the Wood
(Fussion Sonnet)

This staff became a snake before my eyes!
It garnered instant dread
while hung above my head
in forest where I tread,
and one can just imagine my surprise.
I know not how it got up there,
This serpent hanging in the air.
May instincts told me to beware!

Is this the Evil One who tempted EVE?
With God's forbidden fruit, did he deceive?

As I recall old Moses had a staff
that turned into a serpent
when thrown upon the ground
in front of Egypt's Pharaoh.

This staff became a snake before my eyes!
But now I see it's just a branch of wood,
a serpentine display misunderstood.
Be still my heart, there's nothing here to fear!
Its origin is now completely clear.
No staff became a snake before my eyes!
'Twas just a figment caught me by surprise.

Author Notes:

I actually did come across this wooden branch during one of my walks in the woods, and it did startle me for a minute. It is only a wooded vine, but it sure looked like a snake for a moment. Of course, I was inspired to capture its image and write this poem.

The poem is a Fusion Sonnet. This falls under the auspices of the Modern Sonnet genre. As such, it breaks several Sonnet rules. Most notably, it has 21 Lines. The Fusion comes from blending in 4 lines of Free Verse at lines 11 through 14. It has a strict Structure and Rhyme Scheme.

14 line Poem followed by a Half Sonnet of 7 lines acting as a Coda. No particular Meter is followed, "Fusing" it with the modern Free Verse

For more information, see back pages.

Poem 52: Up a Tree
(Triolet)

I thought I saw a bear up there,
   right at the apex of the tree.
I really couldn't help but stare.
I thought I saw a bear up there,
and it was clinging tight, with care.
   But no, it's just a burl I see.
I thought I saw a bear up there,
   right at the apex of the tree.

Author Notes:

When I was out walking on Pike's Island, an island in the Mississippi River just below Fort Snelling, I thought I spotted a black bear up in a tree. It surprised me for a moment, until I realized that it was just a burl. Zebulon Pike camped on this island in 1805 during his expedition after the Louisiana Purchase that resulted in the naming of Pike's Peak in Colorado.

A burl is a growth on a tree. Sources suggest that a burl could be caused by many environmental factors. To be sure, burls and galls may serve as secondary infection avenues for insects and diseases, but as a rule they do not appear to be harmful to most trees and maintain a protective bark around the area where the burl occurs. They look like bumps or warty growths probably caused as a result of some environmental injury.

Whatever the irritation, it stimulates a protective growth as a defense mechanism. Burls can yield a very peculiar and highly figured wood, one prized for its beauty by many and sought after by people such as furniture makers, artists, and wood sculptors.

This poem is a Triolet.

A Triolet is a French repeating poem of only eight lines, and often all lines are in iambic tetrameter. It contains only 2 rhymes, with a rhyme scheme of:

ABaAabAB.

The fourth and seventh lines are the same exact line as the first (see capital As). The eighth line is the same exact line as the second (see capital Bs). Because five of the eight lines repeat, this is one of the easiest French formats to create, yet when the repeated lines are chosen well, it creates a lovely poem.

Poem 53: Uprooted Lives
Quatrains (9-7 Metered)

Deep rooted trees, uprooted,
As wild winds wreak havoc on the ground.
Power lines down, lights are out.
Danger is real! Heed the siren's sound!

Uprooted trees: cleared away

Hard rain pours down in torrents,
As hail plummets to punish below.
Titans clash in lurid flash,
When overwhelmed cauldrons overflow.

Uprooted bridges: are gone

One storm follows another
In a series of soggy ruined days
Yet, between crackling thunders,
Life moves on as we manage to play.

Uprooted plans: slight delay

Chain saws remove the rubble.
Soon downed power lines have been restored.
Mother Nature let us know
That her weather plans can't be ignored.

Uprooted lives: move on

Author Notes

Went camping one weekend: Friday to Sunday.
All three days had severe thunderstorms with high
winds. The picture represents a typical scene on
the nightly news. At the park where I was,
cleanup crews were out every day clearing
downed trees from paths and roads. Only to
repeat the next day. Walking paths were under
water in many places. Firewood was hard to keep
dry. Yet, we managed to do things and make the
best of it. Trying to give the flavor of it here.

This poem is written I Quatrains with 9-Meter
These are poems with a standard 4 line stanza
(Quatrain) with any rhyme scheme, but a meter
similar to the Ballad meter, but with an extra
syllable that is often feminine., and that alternates
between 7 syllable meter and 9 syllables. Usually
in a long-short-long-short sequence.

Chapter 11: Inspired Stories

Have you ever come across a sight that reminds you of a good old story? I have. This chapter really exercised my imagination when I saw the images. Not only did my poetic juices start flowing, but I created characters that my Muse introduced. Some touch upon legends. Some are friendly with rhymes and fables.

There's a deceitful crane outwitted by a crab. There's a family of foxes seeking a church burial. A lost sheep is found. An Indian maiden tragically tries to cross the ice on Lake Superior. Tinkerbelle sprinkles some Fairy dust. There's a turtle legend. I even give Paul Bunyan a dog companion.

I hope these will be entertaining, and that you see what I saw.

Poem 54: The Crane and the Crab
(A Quinquerne)

The Crane and Crab, a tale about turned trust!
Old wily crane, at pond he stood beside
attracts a crab, who asked him why he cried.
The crane heard words two anglers did decide,
to drain the pool to get the fish, they must.

The tale goes on as crab gets fish concerned.
The Crane and Crab, a tale about turned trust,
proposes perfect plan where fates adjust,
if on crane's wings, for transfer, they entrust.
Then angler's methods can be swiftly spurned.

The fish agreed to be flown far away.
So one-by-one the foolish fish were rushed.
The Crane and Crab, a tale about turned trust,
as crane nearby fulfilled his hunger lust,
consuming many in a single day.

The crab requested to be taken too!
At this, the greedy crane became nonplussed,
as crab crawled on and grabbed a feathered tuft.
The Crane and Crab, a tale about turned trust
took to the air, observing carnage view.

Then angry crab claws into crane's neck thrust.
"I'll cut your neck if you don't land," crab said.
"Please spare me, it was only fish are dead."
"OK," said crab. When down, snapped off his head.
The Crane and Crab, a tale about turned trust.

Author Notes:

In this picture of two trees In the first tree, I see what resembles a crab. In the other, I see what looks like some bird, with a long sharp beak at an angle about 7 o'clock, and tall green head feathers. I hope you can see that too! Inspired this story poem about a crane and crab.

This tale is told in many versions, different details, and several languages. The oldest known writing comes from the Panchatantra, an ancient Indian collection in Sanskrit. Aesop told a similar story only the bird is a heron, and the fishermen went to get their nets.

This poem is a Quinquerne.
The Quinquerne uses ten syllables per line of iambic pentameter. It works in multiples of five - five Quintrains of enveloping rhyme (two around three), with the first line repeated as a refrain line cascading line by line through each Quintrain. The rhyme scheme has the "a" rhyme repeated 12 times within the 25 lines. The rhyme scheme is:
Abbba, cAaac, daAad, eaaAe, afffA, where capital letter is the repeated line.

Feminine endings may be employed. For this poem, the refrain was a bit stilted, as each stanza provides a different twist on trust, justifying its reassertion. In stanza one, the crab trusts crane's story. In stanza two, fish, crab, and crane all trust the plan. In stanza three, fish trust the honesty of crane not to harm them. In stanza four, misplaced trust is revealed. Finally, stanza five, crane trusts the crab not to harm. So, this story has many angles that ripple through it.

Poem 55: The Foxes and the Bishop
(A Story Poem in Sestets)

There once was a small fox family
that lived in roots of large oak tree
nearby Medieval built Cathedral Town,
where they could watch the goings-on
at village church and graveyard, yon,
observing human tasks from dusk 'til dawn.

Renauld was oldest, father fox.
His wife, Fiona's crimson locks,
were his most prized and cherished attribute,
but not more loved than their son Tod,
a playful boy, who would maraud
the local vineyard - Church's precious fruit.

This annoyed the Bishop!

Deprived of wine, the Bishop prayed,
like Solomon's similar raid,
"Lord, catch the foxes that ruin the vineyard."
With that some deadly traps were set,
where Tod was caught within a net.
Then killed by hunters. Body left to disregard.
Fiona was beside herself!
Renauld had lost his mental health,
and these became the couple's darkest days.
But once they both regained their nerves,
determined their son's death deserves
to be respected, just like human ways.

This involved the Bishop.

Back in those days, a fox could talk.
Renauld was soon induced to walk
to obtain a burial for his son
within the local cemetery,
complete with sacred ceremony.
As such befits a most beloved one.

The fox achieved an interview
with Bishop, firm in Pontiff's pew,
who said, "Dear friend, you must be too confused.
No foxes can be buried here!
The Catechism's words are clear –
Just humans, sacred grounds. Request refused!"

Thus invoked the Bishop.

Fiona and Renauld were mad.
The situation very sad.
They put forth a magical inclination.
If humanity is required,
they had the means that were desired,
for foxes were well known for
transformation.

Renauld changed Tod into a boy.
Required further for this ploy
were artifacts of Christianity.
Such things were needed to be found
for access onto sacred ground.
Deception had become a certainty –

to hoodwink the Bishop

So into church the couple drew,
to search each corner, every pew,
and there they found a holy locket chain.
Then, in the village, out to dry,
a peasant's garments, foxes spy.
So into pocket, locket chain was lain.

Tod's body later, gotten dressed,
when found where roads crossed east
and west,
was taken to the local undertaker.
No relatives at all respond.
Considered Christian vagabond.
Consigned to cemetery, pauper's acre.

To be blessed by Bishop.

So, one fine morning, it was done.
To satisfy most everyone,
a small procession exited the church,
that carried a small wooden box.
Inside it was the transformed fox.
Unseen, its true identities emerge.

And on a tree nearby the site,
two foxes watch it with delight.
Tod buried, with all proper dignity,
will hence be mourned with loving cries,
each evening as the twilight dies,
to echo now throughout eternity,

and heard by the Bishop.

Poem 56: The Lost Sheep
(ABAB Quatrains)

Little Bo Peep has lost her sheep,
But I think that I found him
Buried deep and fast asleep
In the forest, like a tree limb.

She left him alone. He never came home.
His survival was looking dim.
That Little Bo Peep can only bemoan
When he entered a tree on a whim.

Poor little lamb was caught in the core
When the bark enclosed around him.
Forevermore, he's part of the lore
In the tales of the Brothers Grimm.

Author Notes:

I spotted this tree trunk deep in the woods. The imperfections in the bark reminded me of a lamb or a bunny stuck in the tree. Look at the left side bark. So I wrote this little poem that adds to the Little Bo Peep Fairy Tale.

This poem is simply abab rhymed Quatrains. I tried to match the meter of the original fairy tale as much as possible.

Poem 57: Maiden in the Ice
(ABCB Quatrains)

Legend tells the story,
The Maiden in the ice.
She met a frozen fate.
Took a risk, paid the price.

Superior's winters
Can freeze up a whole bay.
Save a lot of travel
By crossing it, some say.

Much to her sad regret
Maiden took bad advice,
Started walking one day
Across the frozen ice.

Fell right through a thin spot
And came out soaking wet.
Then climbed upon a rock.
A place where fate was met.

Superior's howling winds
Stiffened up sodden clothes.
Image now forever
Remains right where she froze.

Author Notes

A maiden frozen in place and time on the shores of Lake Superior. A Story I made up, based on the Image. I was up at Duluth, Minnesota showing a couple of my photographs at an art exhibit. While there, I drove up Lake Superior's North Shore a few miles to shoot some ice pictures. This in one of many I took. The image looked to me like someone frozen on a rock. I just had to write a poem about it. So, here it is.

This poem is written in ABCB Quatrains

These are poems with a standard 4 line stanza (Quatrain) with a rhyme scheme of abcb (skipping), where the first and third line do not rhyme, but the second and fourth do.
Syllable count 6,

Poem 58: Ole Blue
(Free Style)

You've heard the tales of Paul Bunyan
And Babe, his big blue ox.
He also had a big puppy
That grew big as a house.

The puppy was a Saint Bernard
With paws bigger than most
Seen around Lake Superior
Swiming in that big Lake

Now Paul really loved that doggy.
One day while he was about,
Watched it floating in cold water,
He named that doggy Blue.

You probably would have too!

That lake's as cold as the arctic,
With winds that blow huge waves.
A cold cruel death is awaiting
For sinking sailormen.

Once when the winds of November
Sunk a ship off the shore.
Old Blue dove into the water
Saving the entire crew

What a wonderful thing to do!

If you ever see his white head
Around the old ice caves
It just might be Old Blue out swimming
Someday he might save you.

Then you'll know this story is true!

Author Notes

Growing up in Minnesota, I heard lots of tall Lumberjack tales about that giant, Paul Bunyan and Babe the Blue OX. When I took this photograph up in Duluth along Lake Superior, The icy rock on the right looked to me like a big dog swimming in the water. So, I thought I'd add a chapter of my own. After all, I am a Minnesotan, born and bred), to the legends. So, I created another companion for Paul and Babe - Blue, the Saint Brenard. Hope you enjoyed it.

This is a Free Style poem.
A Free Style Poem is a subset of Free Verse, which has no rhyme scheme, tempo, or meter pattern. It just flows with the words. The author adds dimension in how the poem is felt, through the use of pace and pause, created in how the words are arranged on the page. The distinction between Free Style and Free Verse is that Free Style contains some rhyme while Free Verse does not. It rhymes in places as the author wants, but not necessarily consistently.

Poem 59: The Fairy and the Gnome
(A Droighneach Poem)

Tinkerbelle, as fairies will, was chasing waterfalls.
Heard some calls, nearby the falls. Wondering
"Whatever?"
A clever gnome, named Jerome, was spouting protocols,
which soon forestalls an anticipated endeavor.
"The rules," says he, "by most, are meant to be
distinguished
by the established boundaries of these properties."
Made her freeze, with unease, and ask him to embellish,
since gibberish translation exceeds her expertise.

Jerome said, "Well, this tale I tell, about principle
is simple. Do not trespass. This place is spiritual.
It's unusual, but this ground must stay untrampled.
Set an example, and leave it safe and beautiful."
So Tinkerbelle, whose heart was full, sprinkled fairy-dust
with expansive thrust. The earth began to radiate
and accentuate with flowers. Colors readjust
in robust rainbow curves that forever captivate.

From that time on, the story goes,
this special spot, now, always glows.

Author Notes:

I took this image of a waterfall and noticed a reflection, in the water's lower center, something that reminded me of the Fairy, Tinkerbelle. Nearby, and just above, is a pointed rock that shows two eyes and a nose, which made me think of a gnome. From that, this story ensued.

This poem is a Droighneach. Droighneach (dra'iy-nach) Gaelic, is sometimes referred to as "the thorny" because of the degree of difficulty in writing this Gaelic Verse Form that employs cross rhyme and requires 3 syllable end words. It is a traditional Irish quatrain stanza of 9-to-13-syllable lines alternately rimed (abab), always on 3-syllable words, with at least two cross-rimes linking the pair of lines in each half and involving those lines' end-words, plus alliteration in every line, usually between the end-word and the preceding stressed (always the case for a quatrain) last line. Being Irish, it also requires the dunedh, meaning it should end where it began (opening word or phrase or line repeated at the end). See notes in back for further details.

Poem 60: Turtle Tree
(An Englyn Unodle)

Turtle, master of the mud,
during legends of The Flood,
your shell held slimy crud of newborn Earth.
Your worth is ancient blood.

Turtle thoughts, reputed wise.
Shell that shuts when threats arise.
It's no surprise a tortoise lives so long.
So strong, we glamorize.

Turtle, it's your placid pace
that so often wins the race.
You wisely never chase something too fast.
So you last, with grand grace.

Turtle, you are amazing.
Do I see you gently grazing
here, while I'm appraising these tangled root's
attributes, so dazing?

Turtle, image in the wood,
saw you clearly where I stood.
Can't comprehend just how you could be there.
I swear, you're just driftwood.

Author Notes:

Here is another amazing tree root that I found along the Mississippi. Turtles are frequently depicted as easygoing, patient, and wise creatures. Due to their long lifespan, slow movement, sturdiness, and wrinkled appearance, they are an emblem of longevity. They have an important role in mythologies, often in creation myths regarding the origin of the Earth, which describe a large cosmic turtle holding the earth upon its shell, or islands as the back of turtle. Many Native American cultures tell a story of the Great Flood, where a man with supernatural powers sends creatures diving to get mud in order to form new earth. Source: Wikipedia.

This poem is a Englyn Unodle.
A Welsh poetic format comprised of two seven syllable lines, one of ten syllables, and one of six syllables. There is a common rhyme at seventh syllable of the third ten syllable line, and last syllable of the last six syllable line. The last syllable of the ten syllable line assonates or alliterates with the third syllable of six syllable line. So the rhyme scheme of each stanza becomes:
a, a,(a,b),(b,a)
where the lines in parens represent the inline-end line rhyme structure .ayout:
x x x x x x a
x x x x x x a
x x x x x x a x x b
x x b x x a

Chapter 12: Surprising Sights

Unlike the chapter of shocking discoveries, these are more subtle. You look at them and become amazed, or surprised at what you see. Simple sights like a roof, tree roots, vines, a flower or a rock reveal a surprising actuality. Maybe not a shock or a double take, but possibly a smile, or you say, "Hmmm." You just never know what you'll come across when you look.

Poem 61: Dancer
(A Katie21 Poem)

Along
The hills
The plains
He
Dances

To the beat
Of
The Earth
The sound of the wind

Bird songs

Life

Author Notes:

This photograph is of a tree root I found on the Great Plains at Blue Mounds State Park in Southeastern Minnesota. Near the buffalo herd. It looked, amazingly to me, like a dancing Indian spirit. I felt that spirit flow as I drew near. I was one with the earth, wind, and song.

This poem is a Katiem21.
A Katie21 poem is a free verse poem that keys off word count versus syllable count. It must contain exactly 21 words. It can rhyme or not, be about any subject, and punctuation is optional, and skinny stanza style is optional as well.

Skinny stanza style is writing one word per line.

Poem 62: Ice Monster
(Free Style)

Ice Monster

Crawling from the ice
Creature slick and cold
Dripping crystal shards
Legs of frozen mold,
Monster from the deep
Legends from of old

Sacred
Secrets
Say

"Its touch is deadly".

Keep away from me!

Author Notes

Another story from my imagination upon viewing this photograph. It sort of reminded me of a giant spider-like frozen creature crawling along the ice. This is another photograph taken on my Duluth Trip. This ice fromation photograph was taken on Saturday, 3-2-2013 along the North Shore drive.

This is a Free Style Poem.
A Free Style Poem is a subset of Free Verse, which has no rhyme scheme, tempo, or meter pattern. It just flows with the words. The author adds dimension in how the poem is felt, through the use of pace and pause, created in how the words are arranged on the page. The distinction between Free Style and Free Verse is that Free Style contains some rhyme while Free Verse does not. It rhymes in places as the author wants, but not necessarily consistently.

Poem 63: Lively Lily
(A Triolet)

When lively lily brightly shines
Giving a mellow yellow tone,
Amongst its leaves it deftly climbs.
When lively lily brightly shines,
Masterpiece of floral designs,
Its quiet beauty stands alone,
When lively lily brightly shines
Giving a mellow yellow tone.

Author Notes:

A Lily climbs its leaves. Alive and lively. This Lily that I spotted, while out on a walk with my wife, appeared to be grasping and climbing its leaves. So, I made reference to that in this poem.

This poem is a Triolet.
A Triolet is a poem with a fixed format. This one has a syllable structure of 8 counts or tetrameter. It is a poem of only eight lines with a rhyme scheme of only two rhymes (a and b) that can be represented as follows:
ABaAabAB, where the fourth and seventh lines are the same exact line as the first. The eighth line is the same exact line as the second (This is represented by the capital letters shown).
So, it is very important to compose the first two lines carefully so that the entire poem flows well and is enhanced by the repeats.

Poem 64: Snuffling
(6 Line Poem)

Author Notes:

You never know what you'll find when you're out and about. If you are not careful, you might step on or trip over something unexpected. This fallen tree trunk sure looks like an Anteater.

This is a 6 Line Poem
A six line poem is a poem with six structured syllabic lines consisting of 2, 2, 2, 2, 9, 9 syllables. Rhyme optional.
For this poem I chose to rhyme: aabbcc

Snuffle
Sniffle
Rumble
Stumble
Scratching in mud and sniffing at plants
On the menu - juicy little Ants

Poem 65: The Giant's Glasses
(2-3-4-2 Stanzas)

One day
While walking
In the local park,
Past Dark

I saw
A strange shape
That shouldn't be,
Under tree

Hidden
And quite stark,
Really blending
With bark

I took
Two passes,
When I found some
Glasses

Giant
Must have
Dropped them there,
I swear

Very
Long ago,
In the cold snow,
You know

They're big
As branches
On Maple tree,
You see

Glasses
This huge size
Are very rare.
Don't stare!

Let them
Stay right there.

Someone's needing
A pair.

Author Notes:

What giant discarded this huge twisted pair of wire rim glasses in the woods? Oh wait! They're only vines that I mistook.

This is a 2-30402 formatted poem.
A 2-3-4-2 Poem is a syllabic formatted poem based on shot quatrains where each line is limited to a specific number of syllables. So the flow is fast and furious. No meter required. Rhyming optional.
Line 1: 2 syllables
Line 2: 3 Syllables
Line 3: 4 syllables
Line 4: 2 Syllables

Poem 66: The Gnome
(A limerick)

I came upon a sight not far from home
 A rock that looked just like a gnome
A chubby little face
In most unusual place
Could not discern – grimace from a groan

Author Notes:

I see a face with chubby cheeks and as bent hat looking out of this rock. Maybe I have too wild imagination. if you don't see it, imagine the the long crack across the front as eyebrows. and that trapezoid impression as a mouth area with just the hint of lips inside. Just above a dot of a button nose. if you see that, then you should see the hair line and the toppled hat. Chubby cheeks. Almost a Santa. Is he squinting or frowning? Oh well, just having fun.

This poem is a Limerick.
A Limerick is a short, often nonsensical, political or funny, poem.
The typical structure of a Limerick is two long lines of either 8 0r 9 (9 is the most common) syllables syllable, followed by two shorter lines of either 5 or 6 syllables. Then a closing longer line the same count as the first two lines.
The rhyme scheme of most limericks is usually aabba.
There is a lyrical tempo also to each line.
Long line Tempo
da Da /da da Da /da da Da (8 syllables)
da da Da /da da Da /da da Da (9 syllables)
Short line tempo
da Da /da da Da (5 syllables)
da da Da /da da Da (6 syllables)

Poem 67: Uprooted
(5-7-5 Poem)

Author Notes:

Rapid change distorts reality. Even tree roots are running away. Talk about a root, this one is unbelievable. It is located at Harriet Island, just across from downtown St. Paul. It's hard to miss, once you come across it. My Muse ran away with it too.

This is a 5-7-5 formatted poem.
A 5-7-5 formatted poem is an American version of the Japanese Haiku, only without all the formal requirements of a Haiku.As such it contains only 3 lines designated by their syllable count.
Line 1: 5 syllables
Line 2: 7 syllables
Line 3: 5 Syllables
No rhyme or meter required

The World is Changing
Reality is Slipping
Feeling Uprooted

Chapter 13: Late Additions

After I had compiled and organized my known list of Animated Stills, I went through my complete catalog of written poems to see if I had overlooked any that were of this genre that weren't identified as such and found these additional poems. So, I added them here, so as not to disrupt my other categories and poem numbering.

Poem 68: Alien Evidence

(A L'Arora)

There's stories and rumors passed down
that Extra-terrestrials visited Earth
a very long time ago.
Their presence impacted culture.
Their knowledge enhanced society.
Ancient legends tell of it all.
They became the gods of old,
that stories obscurely recall.

One day, I was walking along,
enjoying the woods and the beach
on a path I had often walked
with a large boulder marking the turn.
I'd never before walked behind it,
but today was providing a lull.
As I looked at its back, I was startled.
Not a rock – an alien skull.

I've studied this subject before.
This skull had that classical shape –
with an oversized cranium forehead
that tapers to a narrow chin.
Much like an inverted pear
with a face that the tales portray
about those encounters from space -
 an alien known as a Gray.

Now there right before me it is.
Revealing the hidden unknown.
Like a head from Easter Island,
The Maori stones of the Rapanu,
or the Olmec's colossal heads.
Released of all former pretense.
The proof has been sitting right here.
This skull is Alien evidence.

Author Notes:

Doesn't this huge stone look like an Alien head? I spotted it in the woods where I walk, and have gone passed it many times. This time I approached it from behind, just as described. It will become one of my Animated Stills Collection.

If you are familiar with the TV shows The X Files, or Ancient Aliens, then you know what I mean by a Gray.

This Poem is an A L'Arora.
The A L'Arora is a form created by Laura Lamarca. The A L'Arora is named after her as "La" is her signature. "Aurora" is Italian and means "dawn" - "Arora" is derived from this. It consists of 8-lined stanzas. The rhyme scheme for this form is:

a, b, c, d, e, f, g, f,

with no syllable count per line. The minimum length for the poem is 4 stanzas with no maximum length stipulation. This format combines both the freedom of a Free Verse poem, but adds a tiny bit of structure by stipulating the number of lines, and fixing a rhyme pairing at lines 6 and 8 of each stanza. So you have a hybrid here of both Free Verse and structured rhyming verse.

Poem 69: Dryad's Dance
(Awdl Gwydd)

A willow greets the fading sun,
the day near done, with arms stretched wide.
A wooden maiden, torso spun,
begun when silhouettes subside.

She weeps her greenest tear-dropped leaves.
She grieves the final warm embrace.
A trace of sun, as willow weaves
achieve a golden veil, with grace.

She poses in that hidden vale,
proud Dryad goddess of the green.
Eurydice, seen in father's trail,
a female form in dance, serene.

Her branches raised in fifth en haut,
so taut, she holds at full arret,
leaves set in braided green and gold,
behold this willow's wild ballet.

Author Notes:

In this case, focus on the trunk of the tree. I see a set of crossed legs that instigate a female form with arms raised. The left arm is bent at the elbow. Hope you see it too. The photo was taken just before sunset, when the sun was low and the shadows are long.

Dryad - In Greek mythology, the Dryads are female spirits of nature (nymphs), who preside over the groves and forests. Each one is born with a certain tree over which she watches. A Dryad either lives in a tree, in which case she is called a hamadryad, or close to it. The lives of the Dryads are connected with that of the trees; should the tree perish, then she dies with it. If this is caused by a mortal, the gods will punish him for that deed. The Dryads themselves will also punish any thoughtless mortal who would somehow injure the trees.
Euridice, - (pronounced you-RI-dike), was an oak nymph or one of the daughters of Apollo (the god of music, prophecy, and light, who also drove the sun chariot, 'adopting' the power as god of the Sun from the primordial god Helios). Thus my reference to wanting a final warm embrace in her father's trail.
En Haut - is a reference to a ballet arm position, where the arms are raised with one arm bent at elbow pointing up, and the other tailing out from the shoulder behind.
Arret - a french term used in ballet meaning to hold position in a long pause.

This format is a Modified Awdl Gwydd, wherein the inline rhyme's position floats, and the syllable count changes from 7 to 8. This poem is written in iambic tetrameter where the rhyme in lines 1 and 3 are repeated in line 2 and 4. So the rhyme scheme is a,ab,a,ab - c,cd,c,cd - e,ef,e,ef - g,gh,g,gh.

Poem 70: Evening Prayers
(Quatern)

With setting sun, Earth sings its evening prayers
All living things give blessings for the day
As nightingales break out their song in pairs
The flowers stretch to drink the last sunrays

As dusk creeps in, the worship soon begins,
With setting sun, Earth sings its evening prayers,
And crickets play their leggy violins,
God's creatures pause, relieving daily cares.

The eagles soar, to float on evening airs.
The waterfowl seek quiet place to rest.
With setting sun, Earth sings its evening prayers
Before the world may best lay down to rest.

All gather now, with sunlight nearly gone,
On fragile sphere each organism shares.
They feel the natural cycle moving on.
With setting sun, Earth sings its evening prayers

Author Notes

Do plants and animals feel a union with nature? Does the Earth itself feel something as the sun sets across its face? Sometimes I feel that they do feel something.

This picture gave me a feeling of peace akin to worship. It moved my Muse to create this poem as one of my picture poem collection pieces. It was taken in January 2011 at Mounds Park in St. Paul, Mn.

This poem is a Quatern, a French poem format with four quatrains that use the refrain in the first line of the first stanza, as the second line of the second stanza, the third line of the third stanza, and the last line of the fourth. It is usually written with an 8 syllable count per line, but I have modified it to use 10, so that I could also practice doing iambic pentameter. I think I succeeded.

Poem 71: Golden Eye in Sky
(An Octogram)

Once glimpsed a marvelous sunset.
A golden eye
Had a glow that seemed to beget
A candy sky,
With hovering caramel clouds
That drifted by to please the crowds
Who were lucky enough to spy
A golden eye.

For such a sight, let's not forget,
That words apply
To such a colorful vignette
That floats on by
To peak the curiosity
And render thoughts of poetry
When troubadours identify
A golden eye,

Author Notes:

A lovely sunset turned to gold .This is a sunset I captured one evening. I spotted it behind me through my rearview mirror. I thought that the sun looked like an eye So, I pulled pover to a safe spot, got out and took the shot. It got me waxing poetically.

This poem is an Octogram.
The Octogram is a style of poetry invented by Fanstorian Sally Yocom (S.Yocom). It consists of two stanzas of eight lines each, with a very specific syllable count and rhyme scheme.
Syllable count is: 84848884, repeat on second stanza.
Rhyme scheme: aBabccbB ababddbB, where B repeats same text. No more than 16 lines. Strict iambic meter on all lines.

181

Poem 72: If a Rock Could Talk
(AAAB Quatrains with 10/5 Meter)

What mysteries are written in a stone?
I've often pondered this while I'm alone.
Does it contain secrets of things foreknown?
If a rock could talk.

I see striations on its marbled face,
And evidence of fracture near its base.
Such a hidden history it must trace.
If a rock could talk.

Has it been here since the time Earth was formed?
Was it thrown from volcano as it warmed?
Or, was pressure the mode by which transformed?
If a rock could talk.

What awesome forces played that placed it here,
In vast unknown events of yesteryear?
Was it the same or different atmosphere?
If a rock could talk.

If I touch it, will vibrations reveal
The patient revelations this rock can feel?
Or, just appreciate its raw appeal?
If a rock could talk.

I'll pick a shiny stone to toss in stream,
But kiss it first, then add a wish to dream.
When settled to the bottom, it will gleem.
If a rock could talk.

A simple act that joins the site to me,
Communion of spirituality,
In oneness with the spot's geology.
If a rock could talk.

These things I contemplate while on my walk,
If a rock could talk.

Author Notes:

Well, I do! I often wonder what a rock could tell us, having existed in a spot for millions of years, possibly since the earth began. The wonders, the upheavals, the passage of ages, are all the things a rock would have known.

AAAB Quatrains
This poem is simple aaab Quatrains with 10/5 Meter, where the first three lines are mono-rhymed followed by a repeated refrain. The three lines are in pentameter (10 syllables). The refrain has 5 syllables.

Poem 73: Natural Gender
(ABAA Quatrrains)

The rush of water
or, the rush of blood
No rude surprises
at normal rises

Nature's Yin and Yang
evident sometimes
when cascade sprang
what often hang

No blushes prevail
in this waterfall
in sharpest detail
this torrent is male

Author Notes:

Ahem, let's not be prudish here. This waterfall certainly is aroused, and its gender is clear. I hadn't really noticed it when I took the picture, but it stood out (pardon the pun) once I got it home and enlarged the image. That wasn't the only thing enlarged, I guess. There are many phallic images in nature. This is one.

This poem is written in ABAA Quatrains. These are simply poems written in a standard 4 line stanza (Quatrain) with an abaa rhyme scheme

I used a syllable count of 5 here.

Poem 74: Sun Worship
(Pantuom)

The Forest is nourished by the Sun
As God smiles down on His Creation
All living things, Yes, Every one
Exists at the Creator's Invitation

As God smiles down on His creation
In Deep forest the Tree Tops are High
Exists at the Creator's Invitation
Trees cradle the Sun, low in the Sky

In Deep forest the Tree Tops are High
Taking Holy Heat through bending Bough
Trees cradle the Sun, low in the Sky
That worship as the Ancients allow

Taking Holy Heat through bending Bough
The Forest is nourished by the Sun
That worship as the Ancients allow
All living things, Yes, Every one

Author Notes:

Trees hold up the sun in worship at the end of the day, as nature offers reverent prayers. At least, that is what it looks like to me. Since trees are living organisms, they may worship in ways that humans don't perceive.

This poem is Pantoum.
A Pantoum is a poem that is made up of quatrains with interweaving repeated lines. In that sense, the **Pantoum** is a form of poetry similar to a villanelle. It is composed of a series of quatrains; the second and fourth lines of each stanza are repeated as the first and third lines of the next. This pattern continues for any number of stanzas, except for the final stanza, which differs in the repeating pattern. The first and third lines of the last stanza are the second and fourth of the penultimate; the first line of the poem is the last line of the final stanza, and the third line of the first stanza is the second of the final. Ideally, the meaning of lines shifts when they are repeated although the words remain exactly the same. So, although they are the same words, their meaning is changed. This gives the poem it's intrinsic beauty.
A four-stanza Pantoum is common, (although more may be used) and in the final stanza, you could simply repeat lines one and three from the first stanza, or write new lines.

Poem 75: Virile Weed
(Free Style)

Stand tall,
erect,
you virile weed!

Go fill the sky
with fertile
seed.

Your profile
clearly
shows your
POWER.

Stature
growing
by the hour.

Above tree tops
your image
towers.

Displaying
reproductive need.

To propagate
your ancient
breed.

No other
rival
can compete.

And yet

how sweet
that
yellow flower.

Author Notes:

OK, I just couldn't resist this image. Not sure what it is, but it sure makes a statement. This weed has a way of spreading its seed. As I said earlier, there are many phallic images in nature. This is another one. I modeled the text to mimic that weed.

This poem is written in Free Style. Free Verse poetry is a very open and free flowing form of poetry written without required formats. There is no fixed meter, tempo, or rhyme. The author, instead, paints a poetic picture with the words. The author adds dimension in how the poem is felt, through the use of pace and pause, created in how the words are arranged on the page. This can create very moving thoughts and images. Done correctly, it can turn simple sentences into lovely works of art.

A Free Style Poem is a subset of Free Verse, which has no rhyme scheme, tempo, or meter pattern. It just flows with the words. The distinction between Free Style and Free Verse is that Free Style contains some rhyme while Free Verse does not. It rhymes in places as the author wants, but not necessarily consistently.

Conclusion

Well, I hope that you feel like I do. It was quite a journey. We saw some interesting sights. We had to use our imagination to see some revealing mysteries. It was poetry. It was photography. It was observation of the hidden jewels around us.

There were leaves and vines, branches and roots, bark and burles in the trees. Some posed for us. There were rocks that formed faces, heads, bodies, and inscribed images. There were clouds with eyes, kisses, and colors. Ice gave us dogs, birds, lions, maidens and fish. Waterfalls were so often revealing. Forests walked, partied, got angry, and just watched. We met some interesting characters and heard some interesting stories. Sometimes they danced. Sometimes they sang. Some hid. Some startled. Some were rude and crude. Others were parts of myths and legends.

All in all, it was both a visual and poetic experience. I hope you enjoyed finding them all, or at least trying. I also hope you learned some things about poetry as well. There are many formats. Each has its own unique aspects. I love them all. I hope you discovered their essence and enjoyed them too.

Description of Poetic Formats

1. 1-9-1 Poem – Poem 5

A 1-9-1 Poem is a three line poem that is syllabic. The first line has a word with only 1 syllable. The second line carries a phrase of nine syllables. The last and final line is back to 1 syllable. No meter. Rhyming is optional. Although short. This format can be quite expressive, especially when joined to a picture.

2. 2-3-4-2 Stanzas – Poem 63

A 2-3-4-2 Poem is a syllabic formatted poem based on shot quatrains where each line is limited to a specific number of syllables. So the flow is fast and furious. No meter required. Rhyming optional.
Line 1: 2 syllables
Line 2: 3 Syllables
Line 3: 4 syllables
Line 4: 2 Syllables

3. 6 Line Poem – Poem 62

A 6 line poem is a poem formatted with stanzas of 6 lines. Normally these would be identified as Sestets, but this form also requires a fixed syllable count of: 2-2-2-2-9-9. No meter required. Rhyming optional.

4. AAAB Quatrains – Poem 72

These are simply poems written in a standard 4 line stanza (Quatrain) with an aaab rhyme scheme.

5. AABB Quatrains – Poem 1, Poem 41

These are poems written in a standard 4 line stanza (Quatrain) with a rhyme scheme of aabb (coupled).

6. ABAA Quatrains Poem 73

These are simply poems written in a standard 4 line stanza (Quatrain) with an abaa rhyme scheme

7. ABAB Quatrains – Poem 20, Poem 35, Poem 46, Poem 48, Poem 53

These are poems with a standard 4 line stanza (Quatrain) with a rhyme scheme of abab (alternating).

8. ABCB Quatrains – Poem 22, Poem 54

These are poems with a standard 4 line stanza (Quatrain) with a rhyme scheme of abcb (skipping), where the first and third line do not rhyme, but the second and fourth do.

9. ABCedarian – Poem 29

An ABCedarian poem is one using the 26 letters of the alphabet chronologically. It is a special form of an Acrostic poem in which the initial letters of the words that begin each line of the poem, or stanza, spell out the alphabet, in order. No meter required. Rhyming optional.

10. A L'Arora – Poem 68

The A L'Arora is a form created by Laura Lamarca. The A L'Arora is named after her as "La" is her signature. "Aurora" is Italian and means "dawn" - "Arora" is derived from this. It consists of 8-lined stanzas. The rhyme scheme for this form is:
a, b, c, d, e, f, g, f,
with no syllable count per line. The minimum length for the poem is 4 stanzas with no maximum length stipulation. This format combines both the freedom of a Free Verse poem, but adds a tiny bit of structure by stipulating the number of lines, and fixing a rhyme pairing at lines 6 and 8 of each stanza. So you have a hybrid here of both Free Verse and structured rhyming verse.

11. Awdl Gwydd – Poem 69

 The Awdl Gwydd (pronounced like: owdle gow-widd) is a Welsh poetic format made up of quatrains with a specific rhyme scheme that repeat the end-rhyme of the first and third line as an inline rhyme in the second and fourth. It's important to state that Celtic poetry is based on sound structures to make them easy to remember, with rhyme not as important as repetition, alliteration and rhythm.
Each stanza is a quatrain of seven syllables. Lines two and four rhyme rhyme with each other; lines one and three cross rhyme to form the inline rhyme into either the second, third, fourth, OR fifth syllable of lines two and four. So the rhyme scheme of each stanza becomes:
a, (a,b), c, (c,b),
where the lines in parens rerhyme scheempresent the inline-endline rhyme structure. For example, below I show two stanza layouts where the Xs are just syllables and the letters show the rhyme. The first stanza has the cross rhymes in the third syllable. The second stanza has them in the fifth.

```
x x x x x x a
x x a x x x b
x x x x x x c
x x c x x x b


x x x x x x d
x x x x d x e
x x x x x x f
x x x x f x e
```

12. Ballad – Poem 33

A Ballad is a poem distinguished by its distinctive meter of 8 iambic syllables followed by 6 iambic ones. The long, short cadence makes for a lyrical sense, when combined with the iambic meter. It can be for any number of lines. It is usually used to tell a story. In the Middle Ages, Troubadours were often also known as Balladeers.

13. Dandizette – Poem 27

The Dandizette form was created by Discoveria of Allpoetry.com. It is composed of 3 six line stanzas. The form is partially inspired by the villanelle and features a tricky repetition of 4 refrain lines in the final stanza.
The form is syllabic with a syllable count for the first two stanzas is:
8/6/8/8/6/8.
The last stanza has lines of:
6/6/6/6/8/8 syllables.
The rhyme scheme is:
a,B1,a,b,C1,b, - c,B2,c,d,C2,d - B1,C1,B2,C2,e,e. (The capital letters designate the repeated lines, while the numbers differentiate them from where they were originally located)
The final stanza is composed of lines 2 (B1), 5 (C1), 8 (B2), and 11 (C2) from the previous two stanzas, plus a concluding rhyming couplet. Where they reappear in the last stanza, the four repeated lines should make sense together as well as making sense where they are first used.
Meter is optional.

14. Droighneach – Poem 56

Droighneach (dra'iy-nach) Gaelic, is sometimes referred to as "the thorny" because of the degree of difficulty in writing this Gaelic Verse Form that employs cross rhyme and requires 3 syllable end words. It is a traditional Irish quatrain stanza of 9-to-13-syllable lines alternately rimed (abab), always on 3-syllable words, with at least two cross-rimes linking the pair of lines in each half and involving those lines' end-words, plus alliteration in every line, usually between the end-word and the preceding stressed (always the case for a quatrain) last line. Being Irish, it also requires the dunedh, meaning it should end where it began (opening word or phrase or line repeated at the end).
So again, the elements of the Droighneach are:
-a loose stanzaic form usually written with any number of octaves but it could be quatrains.
-syllabic with each line with 9 to 13 syllables.
-terminated, written with 3 syllable end words.
-rhymed, with alternating end rhyme abab cdcd etc.
-composed with cross rhyme. There are at least two cross-rhymes in each couplet
-and alliteration in each line;
-usually the final word of the line alliterates with the preceding stressed word, this is always true of the last line.
-written with the defining features of most Celtic poems, cywddydd (harmony of sound) and dunadh (beginning and ending the poem with the same word, phrase or

line.)
(x x d) b x x x (x x a)
x x x x a x x x (x x b)
x x x x x b (x x a)
x x x x a x x (x x b)
x x x x x d x x (x x c)
x x x c x x x x x x (x x d)
x x d x x x x x x (x x c)
x x x x c x (d x d)

15. Duodecatain – Poem 21

A duodecatain is a format of my own creation. I searched the internet for anything like it, and didn't find one. So, to the best of my knowledge, I claimed and named it. A decatain is a stanza of ten lines. This format has two, thus the "duo" designation. Here are the rules:

1. The meter is either iambic or trochaic, or a mixture of both.
2. There are two 10 line stanzas followed by a rhyming couplet.
3. The lines are a mix of tetrameter and dimeter with the following syllable counts: 8888444488 8888444488 44
4. The rhyme scheme in each decatain is:
aabbcdcddc (but the rhymes can vary between the stanzas).
5. The couplet rhyme is ee.

16. Englyn Unodie Union – Poem 57

An Englyn Unodle is a Welsh poetic format. It is comprised of two seven syllable lines, one of ten syllables, and one of six syllables. There is a common rhyme at the seventh syllable of the ten syllable line and last syllable of the six syllable line). The last syllable of the ten syllable line assonates or aliterates with the third syllable of six syllable line. There are two types. If the two seven syllables lines are on top, it's a Union (which I have here). If they are at the bottom of the stanza, then its a Crwca. Below I show an example where the Xs are just syllables and the letters show the rhyme. The first stanza is the Union layout, while the second is the Crwca. So the rhyme scheme of each stanza becomes:

a, a,(a,b),(b,a) for the Union, and (a,b),(b,a),a,a for the Crwca.

where the lines in parens represent the inline-endline rhyme structure. For example, below I show two stanza layouts.

Union Layout:
x x x x x x a
x x x x x x a
x x x x x x a x x b
x x b x x a

Crwca Layout:
x x x x x x a x x b
x x b x x a

x x x x x x a
x x x x x x a

17. Etherees – Poem 31
An Etheree is a syllabic format, intended to make a pleasing shape. Therefore, careful attention should be given to the size of the words, so that the outline of the poem forms as straight a line as possible. Jagged edges are not acceptable.
An Etheree has 10 lines with a syllable count of:
1-2-3-4-5-6-7-8-9-10.
When double, the next stanza's syllable count is reversed to:
10-9-8-7-6-5-4-3-2-1.
There is no requirement to rhyme, but a poet can choose to do so.

18. Faux Free Verse – Poem 44
A Faux Free Verse is a poem that is loosely formatted like a Free Verse poem, but is actually rhymed and metered. So it sooks like Free verse on the page, but it actually has rhythm and reeds like a rhymed poem.

19. Free Style – Poem 55, Poem 60, Poem 75
A Free Style Poem is a subset of Free Verse, which has no rhyme scheme, tempo, or meter pattern. It just flows with the words. The author adds dimension in how the poem is felt, through the use of pace and pause, created in how the words are arranged on the page. The distinction between Free Style and Free Verse is that Free Style contains some rhyme while Free Verse does not. It rhymes in places as the author wants, but not necessarily consistently.

20. Free Verse – Poem 28, Poem 39
Free Verse poetry is a very open and free flowing form of poetry written without required formats. There is no fixed meter, tempo, or rhyme. The author, instead, paints a poetic picture with the words. The author adds dimension in how the poem is felt, through the use of pace and pause, created in how the words are arranged on the page. This can create very moving thoughts and images. Done correctly, it can turn simple sentences into lovely works of art.

21. Haiku – Poem 66
The Haiku is a special Japanese Format. A very short form typically characterized by three qualities:
- The essence of haiku is "cutting" (*kiru*). This is often represented by the juxtaposition of two images or ideas and "cutting word" between them, a kind of verbal punctuation mark which signals the moment of separation and colors the manner in which the juxtaposed elements are related.
- Traditional haiku consist of three phrases of 5, 7 and 5 respectively. 17 syllables.
- A seasonal reference, usually drawn from an extensive but defined list of such words.

It can also be written in less than 17 syllables. Commonly a 3, 5, and 3 pattern is used, but anything under 17 syllables is acceptable. Some other aspects of a pure Japanese Haiku are:

No capitals
No rhyming
No alliteration
The formal format of a Haiku title is: haiku (*title*), there the title has no capital letters.

22. Hir a Thoddaid - Poem 10

Hir a Thoddaid is a Welsh Awdl form of poetry. There are twelve Awdl forms. An Awdl is a Welsh ode. This form contains a ten syllable quatrain followed by a Toddaid. A Hir is a set of four Isosyllabic (10 Syllables, no fixed meter) lines with the same mono-rhymed endline. A Thoddaid is the couplet with the cross rhyme aspect. All lines of each stanza, except for the penultimate one, rhyme together in the conventional way. The penultimate line rhymes with them all in an unconventional way - an inline syllable. Furthermore, the word at the end of the penultimate line rhymes with a word somewhere in the middle of the last line. The Hir can have 6 lines, rather than the 4 used here, but all its lines must always mono-rhyme together. Frequently the stanzas are blended together without blank lines between, as I have chosen here, to give it a more Welsh feel.
Once Again,
A poem of either 6 or 8 lines.
Stanzaic: Consisting of a Hir (being either a mono-rhymed quatrain or sestet, and a toddaid which is a couplet with interlaced rhyme.
Isosyllabic: 10 syllables
Rhyme Scheme: aaaa(ab)(ba), where the letters in parens show how the inline rhyme goes.

23. Katie21 – Poem 58

A Katie21 poem is a free verse poem that keys off word count versus syllable count. It must contain exactly 21 words. It can rhyme or not, be about any subject, and punctuation is optional, and skinny stanza style is optional as well.
Skinny stanza style is writing one word per line.

24. Limerick – Poem 64

A Limerick is a short, often nonsensical, political or funny, poem.
The typical structure of a Limerick is two long lines of either 8 0r 9 (9 is the most common) syllables syllable, followed by two shorter lines of either 5 or 6 syllables.
Then a closing longer line the same count as the first two lines.
The rhyme scheme of most limericks is usually aabba.
There is a lyrical tempo also to each line.
Long line Tempo
da Da /da da Da /da da Da (8 syllables)
da da Da /da da Da /da da Da (9 syllables)
Short line tempo
da Da /da da Da (5 syllables)

da da Da /da da Da (6 syllables)

25. Mixed Formats – Poem 24

Mixed, or Combination Format poems are those that contain two or more poetic formats.

26. Nonsense – Poem 3

A Nonsense Poem is a long established tradition in creative writing and is still popular with readers of English language poems. Poetry that has no real meaning and often makes us laugh and think weird things has a unique appeal. A form of nonsense literature usually employing strong prosodic elements like rhythm and rhyme. It is whimsical and humorous in tone and employs some of the techniques of nonsense literature. Limericks are probably the best known form of nonsense verse, although they tend nowadays to be used for bawdy or straightforwardly humorous, rather than nonsensical, effect. Some poems use made up words to describe things, or just to make a nice sound. Lewis Carroll, Edward Lear and Spike Milligan are good authors to read if you like nonsense poetry.

27. Octaves – Poem 17, Poem 32, Poem 49

This format is written in Octaves, or Octrains (8 Lines stanzas), with several choices of meter and rhyme.

28. Octogram – Poem 13, Poem 36, Poem 71

The Octogram is a style of poetry invented by Fanstorian Sally Yocom (S.Yocom). It consists of two stanzas of eight lines each, with a very specific syllable count and rhyme scheme.
Syllable count is: 84848884, repeat on second stanza.
Rhyme scheme: aBabccbB ababddbB, where B repeats same text. No more than 16 lines. Strict iambic meter on all lines.

29. Pantoum – Poem 74

A pantoum is a poem that is made up of quatrains with interweaving repeated lines. In that sense, the **pantoum** is a form of poetry similar to a villanelle. It is composed of a series of quatrains; the second and fourth lines of each stanza are repeated as the first and third lines of the next. This pattern continues for any number of stanzas, except for the final stanza, which differs in the repeating pattern. The first and third lines of the last stanza are the second and fourth of the penultimate; the first line of the poem is the last line of the final stanza, and the third line of the first stanza is the second of the final. Ideally, the meaning of lines shifts when they are repeated although the words remain exactly the same. So, although they are the same words, their meaning is changed. this gives the poem it's intrinsic beauty.

A four-stanza pantoum is common, (although more may be used) and in the final stanza, you could simply repeat lines one and three from the first stanza, or write new lines.

30. Quatern – Poem 70

,A French poem format with four quatrains, that uses the refrain in the first line of the first stanza, as the second line of the second stanza, the third line of the third stanza, and the last line of the fourth. It is usually written with an 8 syllable count per line, but I have modified it to use 10, so that I could also practice doing iambic pentameter

31. Quatrains, 9-7 Meter – Poem 50
These are poems with a standard 4 line stanza (Quatrain) with any rhyme scheme, but a meter similar to the Ballad meter, but with an extra syllable that is often feminine. and that alternates between 7 syllable meter and 9 syllables. Usually in a long-short-long-short sequence.

32. Quatrains, Mixed – Poem 6
A poem that has quatrains whereby each stanza has a different rhyme scheme, such as: aabb,abab, abba, and/or abcb.

33. Quinquerne – Poem 51
A Quinquerne is a creation of Fanstorian, Pantygynt (Jim Bartlett). It uses ten syllables per line of iambic pentameter. The Quinquerne, as its name suggests, works in multiples of five - five Quintrains of enveloping rhyme (two around three), with the first line, repeated as a refrain line cascading line by line through each Quintrain. The rhyme scheme which, unlike the Quatern, is essential with this form. The rhyme scheme is
Abbba, cAaac, daAad, eaaAe, afffA, where the capital letter indicates the repeated line.
Feminine endings may be employed, but would not, however, be stipulated as a requirement of the form.

34. Quintains, Mono rhymed – Poem 43
A Quintain is a poem with stanzas of 5 lines. Also known as a Quintrain, or a Quintet. It can be a single stanza, or many. It can be of any meter or rhyme scheme. Some can be mono-rhymed.

35. Retourne – Poem 38
A Retourne is a poem done in a French style, having a tumbling Refrain. A Refrain is where a line , or several, repeat. In this case, three lines repeat in a tumbling order. Much French verse from the Middle Ages is written with a refrain. However unlike verse of that same period, it is unrhymed which makes it suitable for short narratives.

The Retourne structure is as follows:

- A poem in 16 lines, made up of 4 quatrains.
- Syllabic, 8 syllable lines. No specific meter
- Written with a tumbling refrain. The lines of the first stanza provide the opening refrain for each of the ensuing stanzas.
- Total rhyme scheme is: xABC Axxx Bxxx Cxxx, where tne x is an unrhymed line.
- Unrhymed.

36. Rispetto – Poem 14, Poem 45

A Rispetto, an Italian form of poetry, is a complete poem of two rhymed quatrains with strict meter. The key aspect of a Rispetto involves the rhyme scheme that begins with the standard rhyme in the first stanza, then changes to another in the second. The meter is usually iambic tetrameter with a rhyme scheme of:
abab ccdd.

37. Rondeau – Poem 37

A Rondeau is a fixed form of poetry. It is often used in light or witty poems. It often has fifteen octo - or decasyllabic lines with three stanzas. It usually only has two rhymes (a & b) used in the poem. A word or words from the first part of the first line are used as a refrain ending the second and third stanzas. The rhyme scheme, then, is;
aabba aabR aabbaR.
The format can carry any type of meter or syllable count, as long as it follows the fixed pattern.

38. Septets – Poem 11, Poem 47

A Septet is simply a poem with 7 lines of any style, format, or meter.

39. Sestets – Poem 8, Poem 15, Poem 16, Poem 52

A Sestet is simply a poem with stanzas that have six lines.

40. Sonnet, Alfred Dorn – Poem 42

An Alfred Dorn Sonnet is named after its creator and is distinguished by two Sestets bridged by a Couplet.
The first one is an Italian Sestet, having a Rhyme Scheme of:
abcabc.
The second one is a Sicilian Sestet, taking the Scheme of: aeaeae.
So the entire
Rhyme Scheme becomes:
abcabc dd aeaeae.
Note that the "a" Rhyme is a Linking Rhyme between the 2 Sestets. Written in iambic
Pentameter. The turn (or Volta) is at line 9, as in most Sonnets.

41. Sonnet, English – Poem 4, Poem 9, Poem 26

A traditional English Sonnet is a poem of 14 lines. It follows a strict Rhyme Scheme. It is often about love. It consists of 14 lines, each line containing ten Syllables and is written in iambic Pentameter, in which a pattern of an Unstressed Syllable followed by a Stressed
Syllable is repeated five times. The rhyme scheme in a English Sonnet is:
a-b-a-b, c-d-c-d, e-f-e-f, g-g.
The last two lines are a Rhyming Couplet.

42. Sonnet, Fusion – Poem 61

This falls under the auspices of the Modern Sonnet genre. As such, it breaks several Sonnet rules. Most notably, it has 21 Lines rather than the typical 14. The Fusion comes from blending in 4 lines of Free Verse at lines 11 through 14. It has a strict Structure and

Rhyme Scheme, but is more flexible in the area of Meter. Here are the complex rules:

14 line Poem followed by a Half Sonnet of 7 lines acting as a Coda or Tail to add additional stability to the poem. No particular Meter is followed, "Fusing" it with the modern Free Verse style.

First Fourteen Lines:

Same Rhyme in 1st,5th,9th & 10th Lines.

Same Rhyme in 2nd,3rd & 4th Lines.

Same Rhyme in 6th,7th & 8th lines.

Rhetorical questions in 9th & 10th lines.

Negative and pessimistic note in the first 10 lines.

Free Verse carrying Optimistic Tone in 11th, 12th,13 & 14th Lines.

Volta gradually through 9th, 10th and 11th lines.

Next Seven Lines:-The Half Sonnet acting as a Coda.

Same Rhyme in 16th and 17th lines.

Same Rhyme in 18th and 19th lines.

Volta in the 20th line.

43. Sonnet, Limerick – Poem 2

According to the dictionary, a Limerick Form consists of 5 Lines (two long, followed by two short, and closed by 1 long). The first, second and fifth Lines must have matching lengths of seven to ten Syllables (8 or 9 is most typical). The third and fourth Lines only

have between five and seven Matching Syllables. So there is a bit of flexibility.

The long Cadence is either: da DUM da da DUM da da DuM da; or, da DUM da da DUM da da DUM.

The short cadence is either: da DUM da da DUM; or, da DUM da da DUM da.

The Limerick Sonnet uses a Quintet (5 line) structure with two Closing Couplets rather than one, in order to achieve the classic 14 lines. The Volta comes at the first Couplet

(lines 11 and 12).

The Rhyme Scheme is: aabba ccddc ee ff.

The syllable count is: 9,9,5,5,9 – 8,8,5,5,8- 9,9 – 5,5.

44. Sonnet, Modern – Poem 40

Modern Sonnets, don't necessarily follow the same rules as the more Traditional Sonnets. While there were once Strict Rules about how many Lines could be in a Sonnet, how many Syllables had to be in every Line, and the Rhyme Scheme the Sonnet had to follow, the writers of Modern Sonnets have much more freedom when it comes to Structure, Meter, and Rhyme. It can be difficult to distinguish different types of Modern Sonnets because the purpose of the modern poetry writers who write these types of poems is often to "break the rules." In fact, Modern Sonnets have a lot in common with Free Form, also known as Free Verse, poetry. However, while similar to Free Form Poetry in many ways,

Modern Sonnets tend to have a bit more Structure and will have certain Characteristics that will classify it as a Sonnet.

45. Sonnet, Spenserian – Poem 23

The Spenserian Sonnet is a third Major Type of Sonnet, (along with the Italian and English Sonnets). It was invented in the sixteenth century by the English poet Edmund Spenser. It has the same Structure as the English Sonnet, but it employs a different
Rhyme Scheme of:
abab, bcbc, cdcd, ee,
The "b" Rhyme carries from the first Stanza to the second, while the "c" Rhyme caries from the second to the third Stanza, which links the Rhymes within the three Quatrains together.
This puts less pressure on the final Couplet at the end to resolve the argument. The three Quatrains develop separate ideas, but they are closely related to each other. The Couplet then simply provides a different idea or commentary.The Spenserian Sonnet is written
in iambic Pentameter, like the other two Major Sonnet Forms.

46. Symmetrina – Poem 19

The Symmetrina was created by Fanstorian Pantygynt. I discovered it while reviewing his poem, Polhena Beach, Sri Lanka, 0600.
I chose this format because it undulates too.
It is called it a Symmetrina because it presents a symmetrical shape and rhyme scheme over each stanza: The rhyme scheme for each is:
abcba.
The rhythm is iambic throughout. It is structured in Quintets, which are stanzas with 5 lines. The first and last lines are Alexandrine Hexameters (12 syllables), the second and fourth pentameters (10 syllables) and the third is a tetrameter (8 syllables). So the meter becomes: 12,10,8,10,12.
No limit to the number of stanzas.
For this poem I modified the rhyme scheme a bit. I used the middle unrhymed line c in the middle of the stanza as an interlinked, repeating line in every stanza. I also used the c rhyme as the first and last rhyme in the final stanza to give a somewhat unique overall rhyme scheme that looks like this:
abCba - deCed - cfCfc.

47. Tambour – Poem 12

The Tambour was created by Fanstorian RGstar. A Tambor is a very complex format that uses rhyme and different types of lines to provide pace and rhythm.
"Tambour" = French for drum.
The reason for the title is the fact that the rhythm of the parade drum is incorporated in the poem. If one can visualize a parade walking by and the sound of the drums as they march through. The poetry is set to mimic the sound and roll of the drums.
It uses 3 line types to gain this effect.
1) 'PACE' LINE= offers speed and an injection of emotion, intense or soft.
2) 'COMMAND' LINE = directs an order or a wish for a special action, strong or soft.

3) 'DRUM ROLL' LINE = creates that special rhythm in answer or in influence to the line before.

As far as I could surmise, these three aspects occur within the 10 line stanzas. These are fundamental to the "Tambour" and without using them it is nearly impossible to create it.

The basic form has three different stanza types. The first has ten long lines containing in-line rhyming on most (but not all) lines, and aabb end-line rhyming , followed by short rhyming couplets, until the last stanza, which has 4 lines that echo the earlier couplets.

Pace lines and the short syllable (Command lines) break up the rhythm of your base, or normal, lines, followed directly by a long syllable (Drum roll line) in answer to it or influenced by it. Without these, the Tambour would not be a Tambour.

The PACE lines throughout the poem are very important, because not only do they offer a break of rhythm, but what they contain or what they say are equally as important as syllables and rhythms they make.

There is no fixed meter, just the drum beats and rolls.

48. Tercets – Poem 7, Poem 25

A Tercet is a Poem having three line stanzas. A unit or group of three lines of verse which are rhymed together or have a rhyme scheme that interlaces with an adjoining Tercet. They may have variable meter.

There are several rhyming options, which makes the Tercet very versatile:

aba bcb ded

aba cbc dbd

aab ccb ddb

abb acc add

aba aba aba

aab aac aad

aaa bbb ccc

49. Totem – Poem 18

The verse is somewhat shaped like a totem Pole.

50. Triolet – Poem 60, Poem 65

A Triolet is a poem with a fixed format. This one has a syllable structure of 8 counts or tetrameter. It is a poem of only eight lines with a rhyme scheme of only two rhymes (a and b) that can be represented as follows: ABaAabAB, where the fourth and seventh lines are the same exact line as the first. The eighth line is the same exact line as the second (This is represented by the capital letters shown). So, it is very important to compose the first two lines carefully so that the entire poem flows well and is enhanced by the repeats.

51. Villanelle – Poem 30

A villanelle is a nineteen-line poetic form consisting of five tercets followed by a quatrain. There are two refrains (A1 and A2) and two repeating rhymes (a and b), with the first and third line of the first tercet repeated alternately until the last stanza, which includes both repeated lines. The villanelle is an example of a fixed verse form. It is structured by two repeating rhymes and two refrains: the first line of the first stanza serves as the last line of the second and fourth stanzas, and the third line of the first stanza serves as the last line of the third and fifth stanzas.

The rhyme-and-refrain pattern of the villanelle can be schematized as:

(A1)b(A2) ab(A1) ab(A2) ab(A1) ab(A2) ab(A1)(A2)

where letters ("a" and "b") indicate the two rhyme sounds, upper case indicates a refrain ("A"), and superscript numerals (1 and 2) indicate Refrain A1 and Refrain A2. There is no specific meter required for a Villanelle.

52. Whitney – Poem 34

The Whitney poem format was created by Betty Ann Whitney. This is a seven-line versed poem based on Japanese patterns
with a fixed syllable format that contains 3, 4, 3, 4, 3, 4, 7 syllables respectively.
No rhyme scheme is required, but may be incorporated if desired.

Glossary of Poetry Types

1. 1-9-1 Poem – Poem 5
2. 2-3-4-2 Stanzas – Poem 63
3. 6 Line Poem – Poem 62
4. AAAB Quatrains – Poem 72
5. AABB Quatrains – Poem 1, Poem 41
6. ABAA Quatrains – Poem 73
7. ABAB Quatrains – Poem 20, Poem 35, Poem 46, Poem 48, Poem 53
8. ABCB Quatrains – Poem 22, Poem 54
9. ABCedarian – Poem 29
10. A L'Areora – Poem 68
11. Awdl Gwydd – Poem 69
12. Ballad – Poem 33
13. Dandizette – Poem 27
14. Droighneach – Poem 56
15. Duodecatain – Poem 21
16. Englyn Unodie Union – Poem 57
17. Etherees – Poem 31
18. Faux Free Verse – Poem 44
19. Free Style – Poem 55, Poem 59
20. Free Verse – Poem 28, Poem 39, Poem 75
21. Haiku – Poem 66
22. Hir a Thoddaid - Poem 10
23. Katie21 – Poem 58
24. Limerick – Poem 64
25. Mixed Formats – Poem 24
26. Nonsense – Poem 3
27. Octaves – Poem 17, Poem 32, Poem 49
28. Octogram – Poem 13, Poem 36, Poem 71
29. Pantoum – Poem 74
30. Quatern – Poem 70
31. Quatrains, 9-7 Meter – Poem 50
32. Quatrains, Mixed – Poem 6
33. Quinquerne – Poem 51
34. Quintains, Mono rhymed – Poem 43
35. Retourne – Poem 38
36. Rispetto – Poem 14, Poem 45
37. Rondeau – Poem 37
38. Septets – Poem 11, Poem 47
39. Sestets – Poem 8, Poem 15, Poem 16, Poem 52
40. Sonnet, Alfred Dorn – Poem 42
41. Sonnet, English – Poem 4, Poem 9, Poem 26
42. Sonnet, Fusion – Poem 61
43. Sonnet, Limerick – Poem 2